DATE DUE

MY 22'98			
NO18'98			
JE10'00			
DE18'01			
JE11'03			
DE18'03			
MY21'07			

DEMCO 38-296

Mano/metate and tanque: a living past?, Satevó, 1990

MEXICO'S *SIERRA TARAHUMARA*

A Photohistory of the People of the Edge

By W. Dirk Raat
and George R. Janeček

UNIVERSITY OF OKLAHOMA PRESS : *Norman and London*

For the Talahumali and Their Neighbors
on the Edge of the Sierra
and
To the memory of C. Gregory Crampton

This book is published
with the generous assistance
of Edith Gaylord Harper.

Library of Congress Cataloging-in-Publication Data

Raat, W. Dirk (William Dirk), 1939–
    Mexico's Sierra Tarahumara : a photohistory of the people of the edge / by W. Dirk
Raat and George R. Janeček
        p.   cm.
    Includes bibliographical references and index.
    ISBN 0-8061-2815-1 (alk. paper)
    1. Tarahumara Indians—Social conditions. 2. Tarahumara Mountains (Mex-
ico)—Description and travel. 3. Tarahumara Indians—Social conditions—Pictorial
works. 4. Tarahumara Mountains (Mexico)—Description and travel—Pictorial
works. I. Janeček, George. II. Title.
F1221.T25R33   1996
972'.004974—dc20   95-50961
                                                                            CIP

The paper in this book meets the guidelines for permanence and durability of the
Committee on Production Guidelines for Book Longevity of the Council on Library
Resources, Inc.⊖

CONTENTS

ILLUSTRATIONS

PREFACE

The Rarámuri conceive of the earth as an island surrounded by
a dike, which is guarded by little people known as the *suwé
piréame* (those who live at the edge).

William L. Merrill, Rarámuri Souls

This is a nontraditional history about a most traditional place, the mountain
and canyonland country of southwestern Chihuahua known as the Sierra Tarahumara. It is a historical overview of the people and the land—the first such
work of which I am aware. It is also a testimonial, an eyewitness account,
written and pictorial, that provides an important record of the Sierra Tarahumara in the late twentieth century.

Mexico's Sierra Tarahumara was originally intended to be a simple photohistory of the native people, mestizos, and outsiders who inhabit the uplands,
canyons, and valleys of Chihuahua that serve as the highland watershed for
the Río Conchos and Río Fuerte systems. The task was really quite simple. I
would write the historical narrative and George would furnish the photographs. Where appropriate, I would integrate the photographs with the text.

After traveling together several times into the Sierra, it was obvious to me
that the project would by necessity become more complicated. As planned, I,
the writer, suggested appropriate historical themes to George that he could
then interpret and replicate into a quantifiable, 1/60th-of-a-second image.
Not as planned, I became the keeper of the props and *cargador* first class, in
charge of lugging cameras, film cans, canteens, and tortillas. Finally, and more
important, we both came to realize that we were seeing Mexico through foreign eyes.

George's Czech Republic and my United States are not Mexico, and Mexico is, as the historian Lesley Byrd Simpson has noted, not only different but
diverse, as suggested by the title of his *Many Mexicos*. The Mexico of the Sierra

Tarahumara is not Tijuana, Oaxaca, Akumal, San Miguel de Allende, or any other "very Mexican" place. We came to understand that the Sierra Tarahumara, although in some ways very Mexican, is also outside of Mexico and that Mexico, of course, is a land of rituals influenced by, yet different from, *gringolandia* in the North.

I soon learned that my historian's (read outsider's) desire to approximate objectivity was not always compatible with the ideals of the Tarahumara or the Mexican. As a professional historian I knew that I could only replicate, not duplicate, the past (creating echoes, not facsimiles) and that the present and past impinge on each other. I now discovered that the photographer, too, is not always objective and that camera and subject often influence each other. We found, for example, that the Tarahumara are shy in the presence of the camera. And on one occasion George was reluctant to photograph a religious sect because of his disagreements with the group's leader (or maybe it was simply irritability brought on by thirst, hunger, and fatigue).

In addition, there are differences in approach among photographers. Take, for example, George, who deliberately avoids using color film. He seeks to create black-and-white images *(sol y sombre)*. Max Kozloff, a color photographer, contends that black-and-white imagery "supercharges an inherent sense of drama" and creates "the bleaker photography" that delimits the Mexican reality to a "spectrum of suffering and pity."[1] George would argue instead that the elimination of color from a composition leaves an unencumbered, elemental vision. Including color (an additional element) only succeeds in making the content of an image more complex and eventually distracts the viewer from the basic message.

Both black-and-white and color photographers come from a photographic tradition that, for the most part, is modernist and mechanical, that tends to view time as linear and progressive. In some respects, the camera, the sacred tool of George's being, represents an enemy machine to culture that has negated modernity, or that sees the present and the past as coexisting. The pre-Columbian and colonial worlds are very much alive in the everyday life and the cosmology of the present-day Tarahumara. For them, space and time are not always separate dimensions. In indigenous America people often are born at a place, a color, and a time—not space and time, but space/time. Space, cardinality, cycles of seasons, time, life, and death form a continuous whole.

We were, then, outsiders creating personal testimonies—fragmentary, not total, reality. George's photographs and my text are both subjective statements about the Mexican sense of reality and space/time. The photographs are not "historical"; they are representations of the images in George's mind. And my text, greatly influenced by his impressions and my own philosophical inclinations, is a personal testimony about the human situation in a Mexican context. Basically, both text and photographs speak of collective memories, mythology, and humanity.

And George is, if nothing else, a humanistic photographer. Unlike many investigative photojournalists, George does not exploit his subjects. No trick cameras with a prism and false lens for him. Instead, George confronts his subjects and, through a universal language of respect and understanding, seeks the individual's cooperation. The taking of a photograph is a mutual act in which photographer and subject have participated together, not unlike exchanging gifts.

After photographing an individual, George would often offer him or her a token of friendship. Perhaps a material gift like a sewing kit, a colored scarf, or a Polaroid image (on subsequent visits we would deliver finished proofs of the people themselves, a gesture always appreciated by our Sierra guests). For George, photography is gift giving, an activity that involves personal recognition, friendship, and mutual benefits.

It is not so strange, then, that a work about "people of the edge" utilizes a photographer that has a humanistic approach. Even George's landscapes are filled with people or their activities. Thus while many of the photographic images in this work are symbolic expressions of a living past, most are humanizing and universal. His photographs reveal the Mexican's place not only in the Sierra but also in world society—and how that external "other" has impinged on the cosmos of the people of the edge.

The methodology and approach of this study may annoy some and anger others: the mixing of testimonials, especially the photographs and the anecdotes, with historical narrative is somewhat unorthodox. More important, many historians may argue that to produce a general history of the Sierra Tarahumara is premature since the archival base is so narrow. As a historian I understand the argument, but as a teacher of history I have always been a generalist, and it is in this way that I wish to introduce the people of the

Sierra Tarahumara. It is my hope that this work will serve as an invitation to future historians and scholars who will rewrite and reinterpret the history of the Sierra Tarahumara.

Some anthropologists and cultural geographers may object to an approach that does not tell the story of the Sierra Tarahumara from a Tarahumara point of view, using their words and concepts. They would prefer an alternative genre that would not reduce the Tarahumara to objects being viewed by outsiders. This approach would attempt to express the native voice and would, to a great extent, be based on interviews, quotes, and commentary by the Tarahumara. Such critics would view the photographs, captions, and text as a kind of "neocolonial discourse." Again, we plead guilty, but then I am a historian, not an ethnohistorian, and George is a professional photographer, not an anthropological filmmaker. This is a history of all the people of the Sierra Tarahumara, not simply an account of the Tarahumara. Again, I hope this work will point the way for others—cultural geographers, ethnohistorians, and anthropologists—who, using the latest techniques of oral and participatory history, will create the work that this is not. An alternative genre is simply that—an alternative approach, not the only one.

This is global history writ small in pictorial fashion; a photohistory of the people of the edge. It is about the adventure of living on the peripheries of civilization; about a landscape in which surfaces terminate at the edge of canyons, or in which mountains are the borders of the sky. It is a story about continuity and change. Tarahumaras modify their culture to survive; "outsiders" modify the Sierra and the Tarahumara environment to subsist, endure, and profit in a global capitalist system. Historians, photographers, Rarámuri, Jesuits, mestizos, gringos—we are all acting out our parts while striving to avoid falling off the precipice.

A Brief Word about Organization and Usage

This book is organized into five chapters, with photographs integrated into and following the text. In writing the text, I have attempted to interpret the photographic images both historically and sociologically.

The focus of chapter 1 is historical geography and the impact of the land on the people. The text then follows a rough chronological scheme. Chapter 2 focuses on the Rarámuri, or Tarahumara, and is an essay on pre-Columbian and colonial Mexico that carries the narrative to the present. Chapter 3 treats the role of religion from colonial times to the present. While Tarahumara "pagans," Mormons, and Franciscans appear here, the spiritual stars are the Jesuits. Chapter 4 tells the story of the nineteenth century, during which mining, especially for silver and gold, is a dominant theme. Finally, chapter 5 brings us to the twentieth century, in which the symbol of modern "progress" and nationalism can be found in the history of the railroad, especially the Chihuahua al Pacífico.

The relationship between the terms "Tarahumara" and "Rarámuri" is unclear. The people who are known today in Spanish as Tarahumaras call themselves the Rarámuri. In colonial times they were known as Tarahumaras, perhaps derived from the indigenous word "Talahumali." The term "Rarámuri" (or Ralámuli) is probably derived from "Talahumali" or a common source and did not come into usage until the nineteenth century.[2] Unless otherwise noted, "Rarámuri" and "Tarahumara" are used interchangeably. The singular "Tarahumara" refers to the entire group or nation. The plural "Tarahumaras" is a reference to individuals (e.g., 50,000 Tarahumaras). Some writers, such as Campbell Pennington, speak of the entire region as the Sierra Tarahumar. The more common Sierra Tarahumara is used here.

Concerning place-names and names of Indian missions, contemporary indigenous use has been followed. No current Tarahumara words end in a consonant. The suffix *chic* added to a Tarahumara word is a locative that means "place of." Although seventeenth-century dictionaries had Tarahumara words ending in *c*, the usage was evidently dropped sometime in the eighteenth century. Therefore, for example, "Basaseachic," meaning "place of coyotes," is rendered "Basaseachi" here. Mission towns, called "Tomochic" or "Papigochic" by the missionaries, are herein called "Tomochi" and "Papigochi." The names of most Spanish and Mexican towns, mining camps, and haciendas, even if derived from the Tarahumara language, follow traditional Spanish usage.

In writing the captions for the photographs, every attempt has been made to be accurate and specific in identifying the locale. Sometimes the name of a particular *ranchería* was unknown to us, in which case the general region is given. All individuals are identified when their names were given to us, regardless of ethnicity or nationality. Obviously, those individuals who posed for the camera or gave us their names cooperated with us. If a full name is not given, it is only because the person being photographed preferred to be known by first name, nickname, or surname. This project does differ from others in that no attempt has been made to "protect" the indigenes or "respect" their desire for anonymity. As indicated before, we tried to be good guests and not intrude where the camera was not wanted. Although some informants, Tarahumaras and non-Indians alike (especially members of the army), wanted to remain anonymous, the majority of our informants and subjects did not seek our protection and actively sought contact with "outsiders."

W. DIRK RAAT

Fredonia, New York

ACKNOWLEDGMENTS

Financial support for this project has come from a variety of sources. An early exploratory trip to the Sierra in the mid-1980s was financed by the National Endowment for the Humanities. Two Scholarly Incentive Awards from the Office of the Academic Vice President at the State University of New York (SUNY) at Fredonia (fall 1989 and fall 1994) and four New York State/United University Professions Faculty Travel Grants allowed me to do fieldwork in Chihuahua and library research at the Nettie Lee Benson Latin American Collection at the University of Texas at Austin. The Research Services office at SUNY Fredonia directed by Maggie Bryan-Peterson paid for the costs of photocopying. Sylvia Peterson of the Department of History typed the captions. Polaroid furnished some film for the project.

A primary source of contemporary history comes from oral interviews. Of the several people who helped me most, I must single out Don Bush of La Bufa and his several Tarahumara friends and informants, especially Clemente Figueroa. The anthropologist Jerome M. Levi and Father Luis Verplancken, S.J., were also helpful. Other individuals who shared information with me on the road and in Chihuahua include Jeff Chandler, Liliana M. Carosso, Pedro Martin, Helen Martin, Jim Moss, Karen Yamada, Dennis James Vanbuskirk, Monse Bustillos, Betty Epp, Gene Wilhelm, Daniel González, Margarita Quintero de González, and Alejandrina López Cadena.

Special thanks go to several colleagues. William L. Merrill of the Smithsonian Institution provided invaluable information on Tarahumara religion and willingly shared his expertise concerning the impact of the Jesuits and the Franciscans on the Tarahumara. Susan M. Deeds at Northern Arizona University directed me to colonial literature, and Paul J. Vanderwood at San Diego State University shared information on the Tomochi rebellion. John M. Hart at the University of Houston traveled with me to the Sierra and introduced me to materials on Batopilas (including the thesis of his daughter Lisa). At SUNY Fredonia, William Proweller (Art), Kenneth Mantai (Biology), and Gary Barber (Library) contributed ideas and gave assistance.

Elliot Hendricks from Tucson, Arizona, directed me to materials on Batopilas at the University of New Mexico in Albuquerque and at Washington, D.C. Robert Schmidt, Jr., of the University of Texas at El Paso, provided me with information on the geography of the Sierra Tarahumara. Alma García from Jamestown, New York, a native Mexican, shared information on hotels in Batopilas. Barnie Burns of Native Seed Search in Tucson, Arizona, was the source of a wealth of information concerning conservation issues. I am in the debt, once again, of Charlotte Morse, Instructional Resources Center, SUNY Fredonia, for producing the maps.

The original impetus for this project comes from my mentor and friend, the late C. Gregory Crampton. As a graduate student at the University of Utah, I spent several summers working with Crampton and the National Park Service on the Glen Canyon project. Falling in love with the canyonlands of the American Southwest, I promised myself that some time in the future, when the dissertation was well behind me, I would find my own canyon and do for it what Crampton has done for Glen Canyon and the Grand Canyon of the Colorado River. I found not one canyon but several in the Sierra Tarahumara.

And, of course, a special note of gratitude to all those Tarahumaras, Mexicans, and "outsiders" who were the subjects of George's camera.

Finally, thanks to my traveling companion and friend, George Janecek, who helped to make this dream project a reality. And since George uses images rather than words to communicate, I take the liberty of thanking those mentioned above for him as well.

Mexico's Sierra Tarahumara

A Photohistory of the People of the Edge

CHAPTER ONE

SIERRA TARAHUMARA

Where the Dead Play While the Living Sleep

The Sierra Madre is appropriately massive, just as a Mother Mountain should be. She gives birth to life not only for her residents, but for untold thousands of other Mexicans in the foothills and plains below.

Bernard L. Fontana,
Tarahumara: Where Night Is the Day of the Moon

IN MEXICO, the southern range of the Rocky Mountains is known as the Sierra Madre Occidental. Traveling the Sierra Madre to the southwestern third of Chihuahua, one finds the mountain *(sierra)* and canyon *(barranca)* country of the Sierra Tarahumara. This is the homeland of approximately 50,000 Tarahumaras (see maps 1 and 2).

Geologically, this region is related to the western United States: both the Rocky Mountains and the Sierra Madre were created at the end of the Mesozoic era (over 100 million years ago) when the North American continent experienced a general uplift. Then, in the Cenozoic era (1 million to 60 million years ago), igneous and volcanic formations occurred along with uplifting. This uplifting in conjunction with the flow of swift, sand-filled rivers in an arid environment created narrow canyons throughout the West—from the Glen and Grand Canyon complexes of southern Utah and northern Arizona through the Mogollon Rim system of central Arizona to the Big Bend and Sierra Madre networks of Texas and northern Mexico. Even the amateur rock hound and plant aficionado can note the geologic similarities between parts of the Greater Southwest: the volcanic outcroppings of the Davis Mountains of western Texas and the escarpments surrounding Creel,

Map 1. Mexico and Chihuahua

4

the highland capital of the northern Tarahumara; the pine and juniper forests of the Chisos Mountains and the Sierra Tarahumara; the lowland vegetation of mesquite, agave, ocotillo, and cactus common to both the Big Bend and the Mexican barrancas.

Fewer than 300 air miles southwest of El Paso, Texas, around the village of Tomochi and the Basaseachi ("place of the cascade" in Tarahumara) Falls in southwestern Chihuahua, one finds the northern perimeters of the Sierra Tarahumara. Here the open grasslands country of plains, ranges, and basins give way to the upland and canyonland region of the Sierra Madre Occidental. About 45 air miles south of Tomochi lies Creel, at 7,784 feet. Seventy miles farther south one leaves the Sierra Tarahumara behind and enters the Zona Tepehuán, which is inhabited by close relatives of the Tarahumara (see map 2).

From Creel, an 84-mile drive in a southwesterly direction takes one over dirt roads, through narrow canyon openings, and across riverbeds through several biotic zones to the old silver mining community of Batopilas at 1,650 feet, a town that is the hottest locality in the state. This drive takes one from what was called Alta Tarahumara on the old Department of Labor maps to the Baja Tarahumara—or from the upland country to the bottom of the canyon country. (The Tarahumara Baja, or Lower Tarahumara, also referred to the seventeenth-century extension of Jesuit missions in the eastern lowlands adjacent to the Sierra or Upper Tarahumara.)[1]

By rail, one can travel west from Creel on the Chihuahua al Pacífico through Los Ojitos, at 8,071 feet the highest point along the line between Chihuahua City in the east and Los Mochis to the west, continuing beyond the Barrancas Lookout (Divisadero Barrancas), through the little town of Cuiteco perched among apple orchards on the canyon slope, to the Bahuichivo train station. Here the Hotel Misión bus will pick up travelers for the 7-mile trip to Cerocahui, at 5,000 feet a spectacular mountain village that overlooks the long winding road to the Urique River below the colonial silver mining town of the same name. Again one is back in the heartland of the Sierra Tarahumara (map 2).

The Tarahumara highlands are bounded on all sides by tributaries, streams, and rivers. The northern uplands are drained by the Ríos Papigochi and Tomochi and the Río Basaseachi (plus the Ríos Candameña and Morís), which empty into the Gulf of California via the Yaqui and Mayo rivers, respectively.

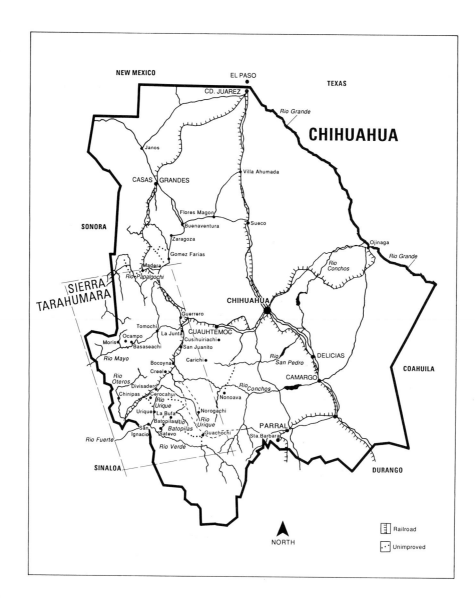

NEW MEXICO

EL PASO

TEXAS

CD. JUAREZ

Rio Grande

CHIHUAHUA

Janos

Villa Ahumada

CASAS GRANDES

SONORA

Flores Magon

Buenaventura

Sueco

Ojinaga

Rio Grande

Zaragoza

Gomez Farias

Rio Conchos

Madera

Rio Papalgochi

SIERRA TARAHUMARA

Guerrero

CHIHUAHUA

Tomochi

La Junta

CUAUHTEMOC

Ocampo

Moris

Basaseachi

Cusihuiriachi

San Juanito

Rio Mayo

Bocoyna

Carichi

Rio San Pedro

DELICIAS

Creel

Rio Oteros

Divisadero

Rio Conchos

CAMARGO

Chinipas

Cerocahui

Rio Urique

Nonoava

COAHUILA

Urique

La Bufa

Norogachi

Batopilas

Rio Urique

San Ignacio

Batopilas

Satevo

Guachochi

PARRAL

Sta. Barbara

Rio Fuerte

Rio Verde

SINALOA

DURANGO

NORTH

⊞ Railroad

⋮ Unimproved

Map 2. Chihuahua and the Sierra Tarahumara

This is also the area of the impressive Basaseachi Falls, the largest free-falling waterfall in the hemisphere. The Río Chínipas, flowing almost directly south and located near the Sinaloa-Chihuahua boundary, drains the northwestern part of the Tarahumara area. A branch of the Río Urique, the Río Verde, rises near the border of Durango just south of Tarahumara country. Finally, the eastern highlands are drained by the Río Conchos and its tributaries (see map 3).

Although the barrancas are known popularly to outsiders as the Copper Canyon country, in reality the area is made up of four major gorges, each one over 5,500 feet in depth. Through two of these canyons flows the Río Urique, beginning in the vicinity of Norogachi and entering the Río Fuerte downstream. The upper canyon is also known as the Barranca del Cobre (Copper Canyon) and the lower canyon (starting above the town of Urique), the Barranca del Urique (Urique means "canyon" in Tarahumara; thus the senseless translation of Barranca del Urique as "Canyon Canyon"). The narrow southern gorge, populated by drug traffickers, some Tepehuanes, and a few romantic canyoneers, is the Sinforosa Canyon through which passes the Río Verde, the largest of the three rivers that drain the Sierra Tarahumara. In between is Batopilas Canyon, home to the Cerro Colorado and Batopilas rivers. All of these waters eventually join the Fuerte downstream (map 3).

Like most observers, I usually make the inevitable comparisons of the Sierra Tarahumara with the Grand Canyon of the Colorado. These Mexican *cañones* are wilder and deeper than the Grand Canyon. For example, Urique Canyon is 6,136 feet deep, while the Grand Canyon at Hopi Point is a mere 4,674 feet.[2] Although the two canyon systems share a similar geological past, their differences outweigh their similarities. The terrain is rough and broken in both areas, but the cliff walls of the Sierra Tarahumara are in general less sheer, the colors more diffuse and delicate—the hues being chiefly green, blue, and brown, not the fiery glow of red sandstone that characterizes the Grand Canyon at sunset—and the vegetation more profuse, not just yucca and Mormon tea as in the Grand Canyon but magnolias, oaks, madrones, piñones, cottonwoods, and fig trees. Moreover, the Sierra Tarahumara represents a system of several canyons rather than a single gorge.[3]

But the historical and human differences are what really distinguish the two canyon regions. Unlike the Grand Canyon, which is the locale of only a few indigenous peoples, the Sierra Tarahumara is the homeland of thousands

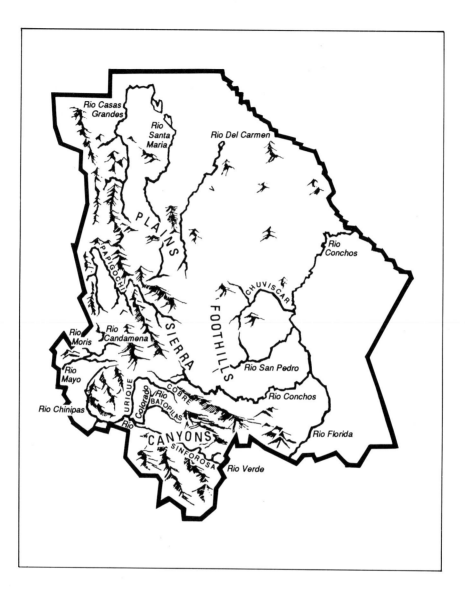

Map 3. Chihuahua and the Sierra Tarahumara: River Systems and Canyons

of Native Americans. In addition, the Sierra Tarahumara is still a part of what the historian Donald Worster calls the pastoral West, an area of miners, farmers, and ranchers that ceased to be a reality in the American West after World War II. Today's American West is a hydraulic West—a land of water engineers, irrigation ditches, canals, hugh concrete dams, hydroelectricity, and big government property and regulations. The Grand Canyon is hemmed in on both sides by the Hoover and Glen Canyon dams. It is true that during the days of Porfirio Díaz in the 1890s an aqueduct ran three miles from the Cerro Colorado to the town of Batopilas, and today there are a few irrigation projects creeping up the Fuerte. Yet the Sierra Tarahumara is still a pastoral reality, a place where there are real Indians and genuine *vaqueros*. This is very unlike the fantasy world of six-guns, wild women, "redskins," and whiskey that dances in the heads of suburban cowboys in Laramie and Cheyenne.[4]

Whatever the comparison, there is no disputing the canyon depths and biotic diversity of the Sierra Tarahumara. Several nineteenth-century travelers and explorers commented on the terrain as they descended the canyons, noting especially the change in climate from the extensive forests and "cool and healthy highlands" to the agave and cactus country below where the sweltering heat belied the descriptions of a supposedly "dry" tropical forest. When the summer rains begin, the highlands not only offer a respite from the torrid barrancas but also supply oak ash as fertilizer for the maize, squash, and bean patches of the mountainsides. This desire to escape the summer heat and winter cold has led, in part, to the transhumant lifestyle of the Tarahumara migrants whose rancherías range throughout the country at varying altitudes.

Historically, the majority of the Tarahumaras inhabited the highlands and midlands, while the Spaniards, at least the miners, lived and worked along the river bottoms. In 1893, Frederick Schwatka spoke of this on his descent into the Urique:

In a little over four hours we dropped from the land of the pine to the land of the palm, and this too on mule-back, a feat that could be performed in few countries outside of Mexico. We were now out of the land of wild forests and wild men, back again among Mexican civilization, but of a kind almost unknown to the outside world, although one of the richest mining districts and one of the oldest points of colonization on the North American continent.[5]

Like Schwatka, even the most casual observer could not and cannot help but note the changing landscape. Grant Shepherd, son of the Batopilas mining magnate Alexander Robey Shepherd, writing in 1937 and remembering his trip with his father fifty-seven years earlier, noted,

If we look backward and very decidedly upward, we can see the edge of the pine-covered bluff from which we departed three hours previously. Between that spot and our present location on the banks of the river we have passed through pine timber, then oak, then scrub oak, next small semi-tropical growth, largely inhabited by thorns [yuccas], and finally onto the region of cactus of varying sizes, shapes, and general pestiferousness.[6]

Early explorers also commented on the bounty of nature, its profuseness of flora and fauna. Traveling through the Sierra in 1890 on an expedition financed by Chicago newspapers, Schwatka, after dutifully listing varieties of plant species, including the strawberry tree (madrones), oaks of different kinds, and groups of pines in clusters that would make good mast timber, said that "the great coniferous forest of the northern part of the Sierra Madre range of Mexico is probably one of the largest in the world (it is undoubtedly the largest virgin forest on either continent)."[7]

Similarly, the physician, naturalist, and self-taught ornithologist William Henry Bergtold noted while on a hunting trip into the southern Tarahumara country in 1903 that "anyone at all interested in nature is at once keenly alive to all the strange life about him; new trees, new flowers, new birds, new reptiles." He went on to say, "One of my strongest impressions is the abundance, beauty, and variety of flowers in the region we traversed. We passed a cliff covered with green resurrections, a tapestry of the most exquisite texture and shade, a gently waving surface of soft, glistening green."[8]

The early explorers testified to the abundance and diversity of wildlife one hundred years ago when the wilderness of the Sierra Madre (akin to the foothills of the Sierra Nevada of the American West at that time) had not been penetrated by the usually destructive forces of the industrial revolution. All turn-of-the-century adventurers supported the observations made by Carl Lumholtz, the mentor of Sierra explorers and naturalists, on his several trips through the Sierra Tarahumara in the 1890s. He recorded seeing eagles, hawks, turkeys, blackbirds, crows, and woodpeckers. And while he admitted that "animal life is not particularly plentiful in the sierra [in the context of the late nineteenth century], still deer, bears, and mountain lions are fairly common, and there are many kinds of squirrels and rats."[9] Lumholtz, Schwatka, and Bergtold observed parrots, white-tailed deer, mountain lions, jaguars, and fresh signs of bears, both the black and the grizzly. As Bergtold enthused, "Let me tell you that I never saw such an abundance of bear sign anywhere as I did about our camp on the mesa, where they come to feed in the fall on berries."[10]

Conservationists and wildlife experts are generally in agreement that the biota of the Sierra Tarahumara, while still quite diverse today, is not as rich and abundant or distinct as it was one hundred years ago. Of the 22,000 higher plant species in the world today, 13,000 of them can be found in the conifer-oak and dry tropical forests of the Sierra Tarahumara. Today throughout the barrancas one can find reptiles ranging from the rock rattlesnake at the higher altitudes to the beaded lizard and garter snake in the tropics. Bird sightings still include a variety of woodpeckers, hummingbirds, owls, magpies, ravens, quail, and hawks. And mammals range from squirrels, gophers, and rodents to bobcats, raccoons, and river otters. Peter Siminski, who compiled an inventory of barranca wildlife for the Copper Canyon Lodge, lists no less than twenty-three varieties of reptiles, fifty-nine different types of birds, and twenty-four mammals, including the seldom seen jaguar, as permanent residents of the Sierra Tarahumara.

Yet Siminski's tally is a bit skewed. Some of the animals on his list have disappeared. For example, the gregarious coati (or coatimundi; known to the Tarahumara as *Chulango*), a kind of ringtail cat that resembles the raccoon in appearance but differs in its slenderer body and longer snout, was relatively abundant until recently. When Mexican settlers in the twentieth century introduced the rifle to the middle portions of the western canyon slopes, the coati vanished.

Although during a 1990 expedition George and I saw a flock of Amazon greenhead parrots, the scene was considered so rare that our guide swore us to secrecy concerning its whereabouts (since we had no idea where we were, the oath was unnecessary). In any case, it was obvious that we could not report, as Bergtold did in 1903, that "in the high country the most characteristic bird is the thick-billed parrot, as distinctive of this region as is the magpie of our western plains."[11]

11

Other animals once plentiful but now extinct or nearly extinct are the big-horn sheep, the gray wolf, the mule and white-tailed deer, the Mexican grizzly, the black bear, the mountain lion, and the jaguar. Since most of these animals were used by the Tarahumara as food, their near-extinction has led to changes in the lifestyle of the Indians.

In fact, the material culture of the Tarahumara is intrinsically bound to the physical environment of the Sierra. In addition to cultivating garden crops, fruits, maize, beans, and squash, the Tarahumara supplement their diet with animal and plant food obtained from hunting and gathering. Many bird feathers and natural herbs are important for medicinal purposes as well. The list of plant foods is unending, but it includes piñon nuts, juniper berries, pecans, acorns, wild grapes and strawberries, yucca seeds, wild mint, agave hearts, sotol stems, and prickly pears from the nopal cactus. Not only does the madrone tree furnish a berrylike fruit but its bark and leaves are used as astringent medicines. Varieties of agave, such as the lechuguilla, century plant, and Spanish bayonet, also provide leaf fibers for twine, rope, and baskets, and the roots are used for soap and laxatives.[12]

The relationship between the physical environment and intoxicants is worth noting. While the Tarahumara derive peyote from one of the two species of mescal cactus, it is primarily used for ceremonial purposes. The drink most favored by the Tarahumara is *tesgüino,* a kind of corn beer that is found at all social occasions. They also derive a fruit wine from tall cacti. A few years ago I had the pleasure of sipping a fruity wine that my Mennonite hosts erroneously called cactus wine (it was, in fact, gleaned from lechuguilla). The Mexicans, of course, obtain pulque, a fermented milkish drink, from the century plant or maguey. When this is distilled, one gets the highly intoxicating mescal (if distilled from the agave tequilana in the Jalisco area of Mexico, it is called tequila).

One might think that the variety of intoxicants available to the inhabitants of the Sierra Tarahumara would be sufficient, but the list does not end here. In 1992 I interviewed an old mountain man named Jeff Chandler who lived alone with his dog, Sancho, at La Bufa. As the interview continued into the wee hours of the evening, we proceeded to swig a libation known affectionately as "grizz piss." Jeff was getting cantankerous, drunk, and tired, but I insisted on probing him about the history of the Carmen mine at La Bufa. As the interview continued, Jeff appeared to become more cooperative. It was only in the morning light that I understood I had not been interviewing Jeff at all, but the much more even tempered Sancho. All of this the result of a few jars of pineapple wine.

Wine and song go together in the Sierra as anywhere else. And again the ties between Tarahumara music and the natural world are apparent. Their drums of sheep or goat hide are laced together with agave fiber cordage. The cylinder is made from the wood of the pine tree. The reed flute comes from cane. A musical bow known as the *chaparequi* is played by holding the reed stalk in the mouth and twanging the string (formerly intestines of wild animals; today sheep gut or steel wire) in the manner of a Jew's harp. The bow or stalk comes from the stem of the agave. It is very likely that the use of the chaparequi, known to archaeologists for its antiquity, preadapted the Tarahumara to the violin, which was borrowed from the Spaniards in the seventeenth century.

Tarahumara dwellings have not changed much since the days of Bergtold at the beginning of the twentieth century. He described a Tarahumara cabin in the following manner: "These dwellings were cabins of the roughest sort, no chinking, no doors, no windows, no floor, and no chimney, and the roof of the crudest pole-and-dirt variety, daylight sifting through it as water through a sieve."[13]

Most Tarahumara dwellings are of one room, the outer walls a combination of stone and wooden planks, with a roof of dirt and poles. Most have no chimneys and are open at the roof peaks (unless the roof is flat). Although they are not cliff dwellers today, many Tarahumara are cave dwellers. Mexican farmers and ranchers construct their houses and storage facilities from a variety of materials. Most often their homes are adobe without plaster or stucco, and the storage facilities are made of logs. In the forest country a log cabin serves as a house, with wooden slabs or corrugated iron sheet for the roof (open ended like the Tarahumara houses). Once in a while one will see a house made of stone. In Satevó, on the Batopilas River, the Mexican huts are of adobe, some stuccoed and a few with straw roofs. When it comes to construction materials and techniques, Mexican or Tarahumara, the Sierra provides the visitor with an organic architecture that would thrill followers of Frank Lloyd Wright.

After the silver discovery at Parral in 1631, mining, ranching, and farming soon spread into the Sierra Tarahumara. Along with them came the Jesuit missionaries, some of whom were themselves active miners. This intrusion by Europeans, which led to Indian uprisings and cultural imports that modified the lifestyle of the Tarahumaras, had no lasting effect on the landscape other than the imprint of a few mule trails and mining sites that left pockmarks in their wake.

Historically, the Tarahumara, like most hunting and farming peoples, were not enlightened conservationists and would likely hunt a dangerous rival predator and valued meat source to extinction if their technology permitted. Yet they usually saw themselves as part of their environment and related to it with deep respect. And, in any case, the technology of slash-and-burn agriculture or bow and arrow hunting was quantitatively and conceptually different from the high technology of the Western world.

Not until the twentieth century was the countryside threatened by commercial, mining, and timber interests. The Tarahumara, equal in population to outsiders in 1900, were outnumbered by non-Indians six to one in 1980. The assault began in earnest after the Second World War. Between 1945 and 1948, a one-lane road was cut from Creel to La Bufa, a distance of some sixty-two miles, so that heavy trucks could move the rich copper concentrate from the Carmen mine to the railhead at Creel. Later, when Batopilas started its current revival, the road was continued another twenty miles between La Bufa and Batopilas. In the meantime, a mountain of tailings spilled into the canyon below from the residue of the Bufa mineworks.

By 1993 gold mining interests had cut a road from Batopilas through Satevó to San Ignacio near the Sinaloa border. The new road not only provided a transportation and commercial link for legitimate activities through the bottom of the barranca country for the first time but also undoubtedly increased the activity of drug traffickers. At Batopilas those Mexican children who proudly wear new Adidas shoes owe their good fortune not only to the profits of goat raising but to the *mota* (marijuana) and *goma* (opium) habits of *norteamericanos* as well. Needless to say, all of this poses a threat to the traditional lifestyle of the Tarahumara.

The exploitation of the Sierra increased in 1961 with the inauguration of a new railway line, the Chihuahua al Pacífico, that went through lengthy tunnels (one over 6,000 feet long), over high-span bridges, around U-turns, and underneath concrete arches to connect Creel and the barranca country with Los Mochis on the west coast. Railroad buffs were thrilled and tourists were amazed, while the Tarahumara did the blasting, grading, building, and laying of rail. The forces of modernization had arrived with a vengeance. The Tarahumara were learning that Westerners do not go around trees and canyons, they go through them.

The new transportation facilities have made the area more accessible to new varieties of despoilers. Mormon missionaries and Arizona backpackers, each in their own way religious devotees, barely leave footprints on the landscape but have a great impact on the indigenous people. Tourists and merchants share their annoying habits, from Spanglish to hot dogs and Coca-Cola, with the locals. Drug traffickers grow goma and mota and attract an army of police and soldiers to the canyons. Mexican ranchers take the best land and introduce alcohol and firearms. But the king of plunder and pillage is the timber industry.

In the early 1950s, Dr. Carleton Gajdusek, a U.S. Army physician stationed at Walter Reed Medical Center in Washington, D.C., observed how the railroad from Creel to Chihuahua had found its most profitable freight in the pines along the track and complained that the "Tarahumara are lured to the sawmills at low, almost insignificant, wages, to work at the task of despoiling their native forests." He noted further that "vast forested tracts have been reduced to dry treeless slopes."[14] Today, in the 1990s, the timber industry has exploited the eastern edge of the Tarahumara country in the Río Conchos watershed. Excessive logging and pulping have increased soil erosion and undoubtedly have adversely affected Tarahumara fields and food production. Forestry practices are lax, and the new timber roads not only occupy lands formerly used by the Tarahumara but also bring undesirable side effects such as their increased use by illegal loggers and drug traffickers.

The Tarahumara have their own views on deforestation. In the early 1990s, an anonymous Tarahumara said the following to Romayne Wheeler:

But the invaders see and think differently. To quench their thirst they behave like beasts of prey; They cut down the forests and open the Earth—without respect and with violence. They forget that the Earth is a living body. They cut her up as the whim takes them and leave her gaping breast open. The avaricious among them seek help from him "who lives below" so that he helps them to find the gleam of money.[15]

Until recently the Tarahumara people have retained their numbers and preserved much of their culture. Will they survive the onslaught of civilization? To do so, they must employ the same survival strategies that worked for them in the past: stay isolated, live in scattered homesteads, occupy harsh and undesirable lands, avoid unnecessary contacts with outsiders, maintain social cohesion through the tesgüino network, and keep a sense of humor.

The Tarahumara people will likely survive, but not in their present form. They have migrated about as far west and south as the terrain will permit. Just as the current Tarahumaras are different from their seventeenth-century ancestors, so too will the Tarahumara of tomorrow be different from the Rarámuri of today.

Perhaps a better question is whether residents of Los Angeles, New York, and Mexico City will succumb to the problems of modern, urban society. Can southern Californians continue to "borrow" water from the Colorado River and the Owens Valley? Will New York City be able to overcome the obstacles of the inner city, including drug use, high homicide rates, and an increasing rate of illegitimacy? And what of the Mexico City of tomorrow, can the dilemma of economic growth that contributes to a surging automobile population with the attendant problems of congestion, air contamination, and noise pollution be resolved? Perhaps, as one futurist has noted, urban society is only two weeks away from disaster. The Tarahumara have at least two weeks.

La Bufa, Sierra Tarahumara, 1992

Volcanic outcroppings, Creel, 1990

Bluffs, Creel, 1990

Road to Batopilas, 1993

A pastoral West? Llanos east of Sierra, 1988

21

Road to Batopilas from La Bufa, 1990

Ocotillo and saguaro, Sierra Tarahumara, 1988

Don Bush and "chulango," La Bufa, 1990

Agave lechuguilla, near La Bufa, 1990

Violin, chaparequi, and drum, Copper Canyon Lodge, 1990

Chico's house, near La Bufa, 1990

27

Tailings from copper mine, La Bufa, 1990

28

Lonely house, eastern Sierra on road to Creel, 1992

Chica, Divisadero, 1990

30

Left: Hermanas, near Creel, 1989

Right: Tewé, Creel, 1989

31

Municipio presidente and artifacts, Bocoyna, 1990

Tesgüinada and wooden plow, San Ignacio, 1990

Interior, Chico Nava's house, Bacuseachi near La Bufa, 1990

Young woman, Posada train station, between Divisadero and Creel, 1988

Christ in the Sierra, 1992

Zavala Cruz at San Ignacio, 1990

Teporáca statue, Chihuahua City, 1989

Left: Rejói, Creel, 1988

Right: Mukí, near La Bufa, 1990

Hijo y hijas, near La Bufa, 1990

40

Señora Figueroa and metate, mano and batea, near La Bufa, 1990

Clemente Figueroa, el escultor, Bacuseachi near La Bufa, 1990

Clemente's daughter, near La Bufa, 1990

Clemente Figueroa, near La Bufa, Bacuseachi, 1990

Chico Nava and his drum, La Bufa, 1990

45

Tarahumara corral, near La Bufa, 1990

46

Basket maker, Divisadero, 1990

"Coca-Cola, nada mas," Batopilas, 1990

THE RARÁMURI

Footrunners from the Past

Rain cannot be obtained without tesvino; tesvino cannot be made without corn; and corn cannot grow without rain. This, in a nutshell, is the Tarahumare's view of life.

Carl Lumholtz,
Unknown Mexico

IT WAS 1993, the Year of the Indigenous People, or at least so it was declared by the United Nations. At the World Human Rights Conference in Vienna, the delegates proclaimed the need for a worldwide system of law to protect cultural diversity. The Mexico City director of the Instituto Nacional Indigenista (INI) noted that the fifty-six separate indigenous groups that make up more than 30 percent of the Mexican nation (and 10 percent of the population that speak a native tongue) have the right, under Mexican law and Article 4 of the Constitution of 1917, to live according to their own culture. The law protects and promotes the development of indigenous customs, cultures, and languages (of which Rarámuri is just one of Mexico's sixty spoken indigenous languages). But then in Mexico, as in most of Spanish America, legality must not be confused with reality.

Even the INI, a federal agency run by anthropologists that has its Tarahumara coordinator stationed in Guachochi, has difficulty fulfilling its own charter concerning the preservation of indigenous cultures. While attempting to protect the land rights of the Tarahumara in their confrontations with timber companies and defending the human rights of prisoners at Guachochi, the INI is an agent of assimilation rather than preservation.

To protect the Tarahumara from exploitation by the timber interests, the INI has actively sought to parcel disputed lands into *ejidos,* or community holdings, so that control of lands will be in the hands of the Tarahumara majority rather than individuals, who could more easily be cheated out of their property (in spite of the fact that Tarahumara property rights have been traditionally highly individualistic). Because ejido management and government requires Western skills and legal knowledge, most ejidos tend to come under the control of mestizo outsiders. With the administration of Carlos Salinas de Gortari (1988–1994) privatizing the ejidos and transferring them to commercial interests, it would appear that "ejidoization" will not succeed in preserving Tarahumara lands.

The INI relies on a system of education that trains Tarahumaras to be bilingual teachers *(promotores)* in the community centers. However, the program has had a greater effect on the promotores than on the community. Many of these young teachers have become marginal peoples in their own districts, disapproved of by the traditional Tarahumara because of their assimilated mestizo (Mexican) traits.[1]

If the Tarahumaras' friend, the INI, has been unable to satisfy the intent of the laws concerning indigenes, then very little can be expected from state and municipal authorities dominated by mestizo and outsider interests. The greatest constraint on those who would disrupt Tarahumara culture have not been governmental agencies, the Constitution of 1917, or the traditions of Mexican law, but the Tarahumara themselves.

Until recently, it would appear that the Rarámuri population increased gradually, or at least remained constant, in spite of nearly four hundred years of outsider pressure. According to the geographer Campbell Pennington, in 1678 there were 10,000 Tarahumaras under mission influence, a number that had increased to over 20,000 by 1725. In 1765 the total population was estimated at 33,000, a number not so different from the 30,000 cited by Lumholtz at the end of the nineteenth century. The Indian census of 1945 calculated the population at 44,000, or three mestizos for every Tarahumara. The Smithsonian anthropologist William L. Merrill noted that by 1980, of 56,400 speakers of Rarámuri in Chihuahua, over 16,000 lived outside the Sierra (i.e., 40,400 resided in the Sierra).[2]

All the evidence suggests that the population has remained static from the eighteenth century to the mid-twentieth century, with no proof of a decline due to European diseases (of which smallpox was the big killer) or military slaughter. John Kennedy goes further, asserting that, at least in the Inápuchi area, "personnel changes slightly from year to year and from generation to generation, but the *rancho* population maintains a rough equilibrium"[3] due to a narrow person-land ratio. In other words, the agricultural practices and settlement patterns of the people of the ranchería are basically a type of ecological adaptation in which resources, while not ample, are sufficient for the limited population. Recently, however, the impact of modern medical science has increased longevity, expanding population and placing additional pressure on the marginal lands of the Sierra.

In the four hundred years since contact, the Tarahumara have pushed south and west, occupying new lands, avoiding outsiders, and displacing original Indian residents. Throughout their history, the Tarahumara have reacted to outside pressures—first Spanish, then Mexican, and finally global. Today most Tarahumaras are found in the uplands and canyons of southwestern Chihuahua. In the precontact period before 1600, the Tarahumara not only lived in the uplands along the upper Conchos and along the valleys of the Fuerte but spread throughout the foothills, plains, and basin and range country north and east of the Sierra Tarahumara. In the north they inhabited the upper branches of the Yaqui River, especially the Río Papigochi; to the northeast they extended well beyond the colonial mining center of Cusihuíriachi (often spelled Cusihuiriáchi) to the Río Santa Isabel (about 48 miles south of Chihuahua City today); and to the east they ranged throughout the tributaries of the middle Conchos (as far east as today's city of Valle de Zaragoza west of Lake Toronto; see map 4).

Our understanding of the precontact Tarahumara society is sketchy and contradictory at best. Most of the people of northwestern Mexico at the time of the arrival of the Spaniards (including the neighbors of the Tarahaumara—

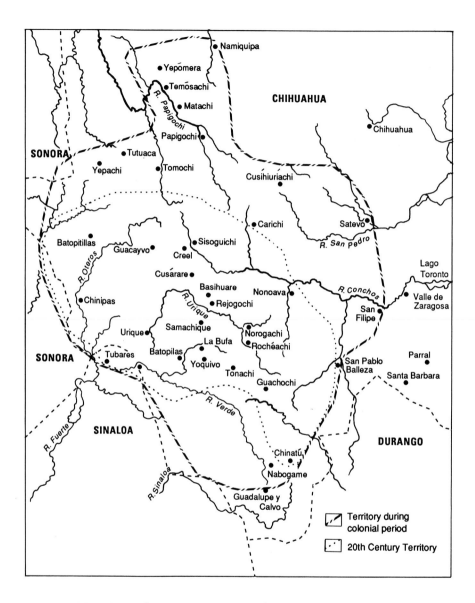

Map 4. Tarahumara Country: Colonial and Modern Eras
Adapted from William L. Merrill, *Rarámuri Souls*, which was adapted from
Campbell W. Pennington, *The Tarahumar of Mexico.*

the Yaqui, Mayo, Pima, and Tepehuán) spoke a version of Uto-Aztecan (with the exception of the Seri of Sonora whose language derived from the Hokan stock). Uto-Aztecan, the parent language, was spoken in an area ranging from Montana and Arizona to central Mexico. The diversity of Uto-Aztecan languages in northwestern Mexico implies to some observers that the speakers of these languages have occupied the region for thousands of years. Yet where some scholars see diversity, John Kennedy and Edward Spicer see homogeneity of culture and similarities of language and therefore conclude that the Tarahumara came to the Sierra fairly recently. Only further study will resolve the conflict.[4]

Fragmentary archaeological evidence suggests that the precontact Tarahumara shared the "primitive" culture of the Basket Maker people of the American Southwest, and at a later period, between A.D. 1000 and 1500, they developed a more complex culture in which horticulture started to displace hunting. These people lived in stone and cave dwellings, wove blankets from agave fiber, used pottery, ground corn with the metate and mano, and made extensive use of cultivated gourds (traits, some of which have deteriorated, that still exist today). In the thirteenth and fourteenth centuries, there were groups of Tarahumara located on the trade route between Casas Grandes in northwestern Chihuahua and Tula in central Mexico, and evidence of their involvement in the Mesoamerican trade has been found.[5]

On the slopes around Satevó, down the Batopilas River, several residence clusters and compact villages have been found, but to date it is not certain whether these sites are precontact.[6] It is even possible that these structures came as late as the nineteenth century as fortifications against Apache depredations. The mestizo politicians in the Sierra Tarahumara seem to know about these and several other locales and decorate their offices with an abundance of ancient artifacts from their region (and perhaps indirectly testify to the antiquity of their office and the legitimacy of their authority).

In spite of the partial nature of the archaeological record, it is almost certain that the Tarahumara in the period between A.D. 1000 and 1600 developed cultural traits that have persisted until today. The most obvious of the aboriginal patterns is the role of the shaman and his cures. The importance of the shaman has endured in spite of the opposition of the Catholic priests. The shaman, who uses dreams as a means of analysis, cures by breathing, singing, and concocting herbal remedies. He (sometimes she) is associated with the most fundamental situations and crises of Tarahumara life, from birth to sickness and death (including burial rituals). He is never related to the Church and its functions.[7]

When performing religious ceremonies, the shamans, like many holy people of the Americas, use the ritual number four, as when the rite calls for the dedication of blood, smoke, and incense to the four directions—east, north, west, and south.[8] Aboriginal (or at least very ancient) instruments used in these fiestas include rattles made from gourds, reeds, cocoons, or deer hooves; a rasping-stick; the flute; and the musical bow (chaparequi, or Jew's-harp).

Native fiestas are also associated with aboriginal life and occur to assure harvests and rain and to cure animals, lands, and people. The liquor used in these fiestas, tesgüino or corn beer, is made from sprouted maize and also predates the coming of the Spaniards. The tesgüino network establishes social contacts for the normally isolated Tarahumara and is a part of a social drinking pattern that involves sexual promiscuity, wife exchanges, business deals, gambling activities (when participants and bystanders bet on the outcome of a flip-ball race), and various recreational activities. Needless to say, the Jesuits oppose, albeit ineffectively, the tesgüino network.

During May 1990, George and I decided to photograph the wonderful pottery made by a Tarahumara woman by the name of Maria Victoria who lived somewhere in the hills of Raramuchi. We drove to the general area and began to ask for directions to her home. After two hours of searching, I was reminded of my earlier days wandering the Navajo reservation looking for Sister Rainwater and getting the runaround from the locals. Eventually we came across a *tesgüinada* party being thrown by the head of the San Ignacio ejido, Señor E. Meza, of the Satepachi rancho in the pueblo of San Ignacio. As a good host and not feeling much pain, he offered us some tesgüino.

George courteously declined but suggested that I, the academic in the group, should consume some for historical and sociological reasons. I did not want to hurt my host's feelings, but suffering from my own brand of ethnocentrism, I had little desire to drink corn beer, especially tesgüino, in which the fermentation process is initiated by baby feces. Knowing that better-known and greater scholars (Carl Lumholtz, William Merrill, and John Kennedy) had already provided plenty of testimony concerning the delights of consuming tesgüino, I immediately changed the subject by showing my admiration for an old wooden plow lying next to the Meza household. Instantly several Tarahumaras, also in reasonably painless condition, sped away to their ranchos and returned with their own wooden plows. Eventually George and I exchanged several pesos for one of the plows.

We were never able to photograph the potter of Raramuchi, but the Tarahumaras, the U.S. customs official at the border, and George's mother were amazed and entertained by our interest in the old, beaten-up wooden plow. Especially George's mother, who could not understand how George would be able to use it to cultivate the tomato garden in his diminutive Salt Lake City plot. In any case, like our Tarahumara hosts, we had succeeded in getting plowed at our first tesgüinada.

Putting aside the aside, let reader and author return to the story at hand, that is, aboriginal influences that have persisted among the Tarahumara. In addition to the material traits of the aboriginal Tarahumaras, such as digging sticks (for planting corn), the agricultural trinity (corn, beans, and squash), pottery, manos and metates, and blankets and sandals, that have survived to the present day, there are the tools of warfare used by the Tarahumaras against their Tepehuán neighbors to the south prior to 1600 and then against Spanish priests and colonists in the 1600s. These included the bow, arrow, and quiver, as well as lances and pikes. Obviously, today these weapons are used sparingly and for hunting and fishing, not warfare. Strangely, the *atlatl* or spear thrower, so typical of the highland Nahuas, was used mostly for fishing. One other aboriginal trait that has persisted is the notion of property rights and inheritance, in which property is private and there is no sex differentiation in ownership and distribution.

It was during the Jesuit era, from 1607 to 1767, that the Tarahumara culture of today was primarily shaped. Most aspects of Tarahumara culture not of pre-Hispanic origin derive from colonial missionary activity. Although the miners and ranchers had an impact far beyond their numbers, they seldom reached the interior. Except for the mines around Cusihuíriachi, Urique, and Batopilas, mining enterprises were limited to the area along the southern and eastern borders of Tarahumara country. The politicians and soldiers, although at the service of the colonists, were often in the Sierra Tarahumara at the behest of the Jesuits.

Spanish traits were sometimes simply added to native practices; at other times they were combined with older elements to create a syncretic mix. In any event, it was usually the Tarahumara, the recipient culture, who did the screening and adapting, usually for religious and economic reasons. In general the Indians responded to Spanish encroachments by incorporating those Spanish ingredients that reinforced their aboriginal lifestyle and retreating, both physically and psychologically, when European intrusions threatened the core of their culture. With the possible exceptions of the Seri of Sonora and the Cocopa of Arizona (near Yuma), no Indian culture of the Greater Southwest is less acculturated and less Hispanicized than that of the Tarahumara.[9]

The Jesuit era began in 1607 when a young missionary, Juan Fonte, attended a peaceful meeting with more than eight hundred Indians in the San Pablo valley, some thirty miles west of the mining town of Santa Barbara in the southeastern Sierra Tarahumara. He had been invited by the Tarahumara in the hope that he could use his influence among the Tepehuanes (with whom he had missionized for seven years) to stop the intertribal warfare then brewing. Unlike the regions farther south, this section of Tarahumara country was first entered by missionaries; miners and colonists did not arrive until the mid-seventeenth century.

Thus Fonte came peacefully, without Spanish arms, and succeeded in bringing an end to the chronic warfare. In describing his *entrada* to Tarahumara country, Fonte, always enthusiastic about the people, said that he "found [them] to be extremely faithful and affable" and described their custom of living in caves, the shyness of the women, and their habit of abandoning or burning the houses of the recently deceased (all characteristics of today's Tarahumara).[10]

The initial thrust came to an end in 1616 when the Tepehuán initiated a rebellion that Spicer has described as "one of the three bloodiest and most destructive Indian attempts to throw off Spanish control in northwestern New Spain."[11] Fonte was killed at the outbreak of the revolt. After two years of fighting, several hundred Spaniards and more than one thousand Indians were dead. Missionary work in the San Pablo valley lapsed until a new silver strike was made at Parral in 1631. The revolt had given the Tarahumara direct experience in the art of organized resistance.

With the opening of Parral, the mining frontier moved northward beyond Santa Barbara. The miners sought to develop the Parral mines with Tarahumara labor—some voluntary, others the result of enslavement, forcible recruitment, kidnapping, and the *repartimiento,* a legal device used by the state to draft laborers for the mines and ranches.

The missionaries now continued their work with the Tarahumara, initiating the *reducción,* or compact mission village, as a means for "reducing" the pagan to Christianity. This extension of missions, which involved baptizing the Indians and gathering them around the Christian village to work in agriculture and ranching, was restricted to the eastern lowland area around the headwaters of the Río Conchos paralleling the Sierra Madre to the west, what was called in colonial times the Tarahumara Baja (see map 5).

Once again rebellion broke out. The first Tarahumara revolt, in 1648, took place in a small Tarahumara community southwest of Parral and was a reaction to the pressures of missionization and mining activity there. Two more revolts, in 1650 and 1652, took place in Upper Tarahumara (map 5) in the heavily populated region of the Río Papigochi in northwestern Tarahumara country where the government had recently established the town of Villa de Aguilar and the Jesuits the mission of La Purísima Concepción de Papigochi. Together the three rebellions signaled a resistance to Spanish influence on both the eastern and the northern edges of the Sierra Tarahumara.

While some of the Indian commanders were certainly apostates who had fled from the forced labor conditions of the mines and the missions, a few, like Teporáca, had never declared themselves opposed to Christian belief and were thought by most Jesuits to be reasonable people. Teporáca became the

Map 5. Chihuahua: Principan Indian Groups and Missions
Adapted from Florence and Robert Lister, Chihuahua:
Storehouse of Storms.

major leader as the fighting intensified, and the price of peace for the Tarahu-maras was their surrender of Teporáca and their agreement to his execution. His surrender, and the fighting in general, was indicative of the factionalism that existed among the Tarahumara, for many Indians willingly allied them-selves with the Spaniards. Those Tarahumaras who revolted, unlike the To-bosos and later the Apaches and Navajos, had not rebelled to raid the Span-ish farms and missions but as a reaction to European mistreatment and to protect their land from Spanish encroachment. When the fighting was over, which at one time spread at far east as the Franciscan settlements among the Conchos, the town of Villa de Aguilar had been destroyed and the mission of Papigochi abandoned. The Spanish advance into the Upper Tarahumara ter-ritory had been delayed for at least twenty years.[12]

Peace prevailed from 1652 until 1690. It was broken, once again, when the mining frontier moved back into the northern country with the discov-ery of silver at Cusihuíriachi in the Upper Tarahumara. Anti-Spanish feel-ings centered in the area of the mission town of Yepómera in the Río Papigo-chi country, where a rebellion broke out in 1690 which eventually spread south to the mission centers of Tomochi and Sisoguichi before it was over in 1698 (two hundred years later a mestizo insurrection would take place at Tomochi). The revolt of 1697, which had seen the Tarahumara die before they would surrender, was the largest of the Tarahumara uprisings and also the last.[13]

The eighteenth century witnessed no uprisings, only small-scale raiding and the physical and psychological withdrawal of many of the Tarahumaras. Con-tinuing was the differentiation between *gentiles* (apostates, heathens) and *ba-utizados* (nominal Christian Indians). Both groups, however, would integrate elements of Spanish culture into their material lives, especially the adapta-tion of sheep and goats and the weaving of wool as aspects of their native economies. In 1767 the Jesuits were expelled from the New World by order of the king of Spain. The first Jesuit era was over.[14]

Throughout the Jesuit era, the missionary ideal of reducción went unreal-ized in the Sierra. Instead, the Tarahumaras adapted the Jesuits' idea of a mis-sion-centered population to their own kind of community life. In the Sierra

Tarahumara this meant rancherías as well as scattered pueblos, gentiles as well as bautizados.

Gentiles, also known as Simaroni, derived from *cimarrones,* meaning "wild ones," usually live in isolated rancherías and are located downstream in the barrancas and canyons of the Sierra Tarahumara in what is very inhospitable country for most outsiders. Contrary to the view of an earlier generation of anthropologists, they were not Indians who had been isolated and had refused to become Christianized (and were somehow a kind of pristine, aboriginal type). The contemporary Simaroni are descendants of renegades who fled from the missions and the mines and sequestered themselves in dispersed communities in inaccessible barrancas.[15] They were Christianized Indians who became apostates. As the Jesuit José María Miqueo reported in 1745 from Yoquivo,

These canyons are the common refuge of those who have fled other missions; and accordingly, the majority of the gentiles . . . are not gentiles originally, but children or descendants of bad Christians who, fleeing the pueblos or work in the mines, have multiplied themselves, leaving their children with an abhorrence for the pueblos and the Spaniards . . . and even a revulsion for the ministers of God.

And, Miqueo continued, both baptized and gentile Rarámuri adopted the Crucifix, rosary, and sacraments in imitation of the Catholic church and considered their own shamans to be as effective as the priests.[16]

The bautizados, also known as Pagótuame, distinguish themselves from gentiles as well as mestizos. They usually live upriver where the majority of the missions were located during colonial times and consider themselves *poblanos,* that is, residents of pueblos or church and community centers. Most, however, are not resident in the towns but reside in dispersed rancherías that belong to the pueblo. For example, the various homesteads at Rejogochi belong to the pueblo of Basíhuare, a mestizo settlement about 6 miles to the north.[17] Pueblos are defined by government workers as church centers and, in addition to a church, may contain a store, a primary school, a jail, and, in some instances, a clinic.

The basic settlement pattern of most gentiles and many bautizados is the ranchería, a dispersed grouping of families in relative proximity. These household clusters usually consist of one or more one-room houses (made of logs, boards, and stone), one or two storage bins, and a small *patio* for dancing. Inside the house on the dirt floor are a few furnishings, always the mano and metate for grinding the corn and the *batea*, or tray, for catching the ground corn from the lower end of the metate, as well as some storage facilities (a few pots, straw baskets, and crude wooden chests). Extra clothing is rare. Typical men's attire consists of breechclout, headband, and sandals; women wear from one to five cotton skirts held in place by a woven sash, with headgear and footgear similar to men. A rough wool blanket or some fiber mats, either inside or outside, serve as bedding.

The most important possessions are stored in the outside bins. Nearby may be a mobile corral made from logs for penning sheep and goats. Periodically this is moved around the mesa so as to distribute and scatter the fertilizer. The inhabitants may have another residence, often a rock shelter, that they will visit, either as an adjustment to the season or as a place where their animals can be grazed or wood can be gathered. A nuclear family of four or five may inhabit the main residence (usually, but not always, monogamous; sometimes, but seldom, matrilocal); other family members live in nearby houses. Large rancherías may have as many as fifteen or twenty houses, but five or six is more typical.[18]

Stone must be removed from most areas before they can be inhabited. This stone is often used to fence off the boundaries of a garden and to build terraces and reservoirs. Stone is also used for fireplaces and chimneys and for storage structures. Some of the Tarahumara become very expert in chiseling stone, especially now that the outsider has introduced steel tools such as the knife, machete, and ax. Clemente Figueroa, a Tarahumara associate of mine, even sculpts busts from the volcanic rock that is abundant in the Bufa area.

The agricultural complex of the Tarahumara has been greatly modified since precontact times. A traditional milpa, or in Rarámuri, *mahuechi*, is a swidden field cultivated by slash-and-burn techniques that will yield crops for a two- to three-year period. The digging stick is used for planting. In many areas of the Sierra, digging-stick horticulture (with subsidiary hunting and gathering) has been replaced by stock raising and, following the introduction of oxen, plow agriculture (the latter called *wasachike* by the Tarahumara). Goats, sheep, and cattle are valued for their fertilizer, sheep are prized for their wool. These animals are not ordinarily used for meat or milk; animal sacrifices are offered at fiesta time.[19]

Horses are not highly prized by the Tarahumara, who spend much of their lives in the steep, rugged canyons of the Sierra. They are considered pack animals, or, at best, ornaments for mestizos and Europeanized Indians. This lack of esteem is partly due to the fact that most Tarahumaras have greater stamina than horses. While a good horse may travel thirty miles in a day, some Tarahumaras can cover one hundred miles in less than twenty-four hours. In late August 1993, for example, three Tarahumaras from villages near Batopilas and Panalachi placed first, second, and fifth in the Leadville 100—a hundred-mile race in Colorado that is considered by running aficionados the toughest race in the world (the first-place finish was timed at 20:2:33). According to Lumholtz, Tarahumara footrunners have been known to cover a distance of six hundred miles in five days.[20]

With the European animals have come European crops—wheat, apples, oranges—but corn (for tortillas, tamales, pinole, and atole), beans, and squash remain the most important food items. Thus while the European has taken the best lands from the Indians, they have also provided them with domestic animals, tools, and seeds for working the remaining land.[21]

Tarahumara religion is a mixture of Spanish and Indian beliefs, rites, and practices, including the pattern of the church or pueblo meeting place. This syncretism is no more apparent than in the Tarahumara deities, Father Sun and Mother Moon (Onorúame and Iyerúgame), also known as God and the Virgin Mary. Father Sun and Mother Moon are associated with the Morning Star. For some Christianized Indians, these three form a divine trilogy, although the idea of the Trinity, so central to Christianity, is not well developed. The Christian fiesta includes animal sacrifice, all-night dancing, the use of incense and tesgüino, and dedications to the four directions. It would appear that the Church fiesta, instead of being the model for the Tarahumara, was instead adapted to the native fiesta.[22]

Epiphany, one of the three most important Christian festivals in the Sierra (the others are the Feast of Guadalupe in December and Holy Week, or Semana Santa, at Easter time), observed on 6 January, marks the ending of the Christmas season and commemorates the manifestation of Christ to the gentiles in the person of the Magi. The Tarahumara celebrate Epiphany, as they do Christmas and other festivals (with the exception of Holy Week), by drinking tesgüino and performing dances to the accompaniment of violin and guitar music (the latter are Jesuit introductions).[23] *Matachines,* that is, eight or more brightly costumed men wearing wooden headdresses and carrying wands and rattles, will dance in fast tempo at various intervals throughout the night to the tune of the violin and guitar. Matachine dancing is completely foreign to the native dance patterns and was obviously introduced by European missionaries to gain control over at least one phase of the Tarahumara lifestyle.[24]

Of the various church fiestas, Semana Santa stands out as the most distinctive of Christian events. Like the other Church festivals, it is ignored by the gentile population (although the anthropologist Jerome Levi reports that the gentiles at Satevó, instead of wearing the white face of the typical Pharisee, or *fariseo,* paint their faces black so as to deliberately oppose and ridicule traditional Christian practices).[25]

Even though Holy Week is a time for Catholic ceremonies, indigenous elements have survived. The Judas figures (exuding sexuality with their oversized penises) used to celebrate the holiday are obvious fertility symbols. Other Tarahumara practices frowned on by the Jesuits include, in addition to the use of tesgüino, the violation of the sanctuary of church buildings by drumming and dancing and the restrictions on participation of Catholic priests in the proceedings.[26]

During Semana Santa, the Pharisees daub their torsos and legs with white clay paint and, armed with lances, do mock battle with soldiers (lancers, archers, etc.), the upholders of tradition. The marches and dances that continue throughout Easter week are done to the music of drums and flutes. If the dancing of winter is the dancing of matachines, then the dancing of spring (and harvesting, hope, and life) is the dancing of Pharisees. The common denominator, of course, is tesgüino![27]

After the Jesuits were expelled in 1767, the Franciscans were assigned the task of missionizing the Tarahumara. For example, Cusárare (south of Creel) was reestablished by the Franciscans no later than 1791, and in the first half of the nineteenth century the Franciscans founded a church at Basíhuare. Yet the Mexican government and the Church lacked the resources to pacify the northern frontier, and with the secularization of the Franciscan order in 1859, the Tarahumara pueblos and rancherías were left to their own devices. This meant that religion in the pueblos would become even less Christian and more syncretic and, more serious, that the Tarahumara would have to face the encroachments of the mestizos without any missionary defenders. The end of the Apache wars and the liberal land concessions of the Porfirio Díaz regime meant that the Sierra Tarahumara would be inundated for the first time with non-Indians, both mestizos and foreigners.[28]

In the 1890s, Lumholtz could report "that the Mexicans have appropriated all the best land round about, and their extensive and fertile ranches lie all around Guachochic. Toward the east, in the direction of the pueblos of Tónachi and Lagunitas, the broad strip of good arable and pasture land as far as Parral is owned exclusively by Mexicans."[29] Schwatka noted also, in 1893, that the lowland basin and range country and the plains and foothills next to the Sierra had been abandoned by the Tarahumaras to the invading forces of civilization.[30] While non-Indians were roughly equal to Tarahumaras in 1900, by 1980 they outnumbered the Indians by about six to one. The deluge had started.

Relations between Tarahumara and mestizo remain superficial, and each retains an unfavorable stereotype of the other. Tarahumaras refer to the mestizo in particular and non-Indians in general as *chabóchi*, which means "whiskered ones," or more disparagingly, "hairy asses." The Chabochis or Mexicans are thought to be sons of the Devil (who, the shamans say, has only one eye and "plays the guitar, but never the violin, because the bow and the strings form a cross")[31] who, when they die, reside with the Devil and his helpers in the underworld. Unlike the Rarámuri, who are the children of Tata Dios (God), the Chabochis are considered immoral, unscrupulous, and rapists of Tarahumara women. Needless to say, the Mexicans reverse the image: they see themselves as civilized, while the Rarámuri are dirty, inferior, and child-like.[32]

The evidences of "civilization" are everywhere today in the Sierra Tarahumara. Tarahumara women weave fiber baskets while the men make wooden carvings for Mexican and American tourists. Tarahumara potters create ceramic ollas for sale at local stores. Tarahumara lads watch North American commercials on television. And a handsome Rarámuri warrior fondles a bottle of *refresco,* as the voice on the radio next door exclaims, "Coca-Cola, nada más!"

CHAPTER THREE

CAVE DWELLERS, PADRES, AND EVANGELICALS

[The gentiles] have better judgment than most of the Christians; since they rarely leave their canyons, they have the good fortune of not experiencing the bad examples which have perverted the bad Christians.

Padre Joseph Agustín Falcón Mariano,
Franciscan Missionary of Guaguachique (1777)

NACETA'S FATHER was a Tepehuán shaman. Her mother was a Rarámuri peyote healer. Naceta's parents lived in Sisoguichi. It was here that, when she was a small child, her grandmother shared with her the dream of the Heavenly Banquet. The dream had originally occurred many seasons previously and had been passed down orally from generation to generation to her grandmother.

The banquet took place in the pueblo of Chínipas, in the center of the mission church. There, in the middle place, when the Rarámuri were preparing their fields for seeding, the souls, to celebrate Epiphany, consumed the fruits of a recent harvest. Although it was the dream time and very dark, the heavenly beings were guided by the Moon, the Sun of the Night Sky. It was the time when the dead play and work while the living sleep.

Several souls gathered together in a circle on the dirt floor of the mission quarters. Across from each other sat the Ones Who Walk Above, Father Sun and Mother Moon. Morning Star also was in attendance, as were the Ones Who Live Below, the Devil (known as the Annoyer) and the Devil's wife. Attending them were many Rarámuri souls and soldiers who assisted in the preparation and serving of food and drink.

In addition, the important religious figures and governors were there, including the crafty General Ignatius, head of the pope's Army of Jesus, and the pious Francis of Assisi. The Archangel appeared in the form of a silver salamander, while the very plainly dressed Mennon was accompanied by a variety of Pentecostals, Evangelicals, and other sons of Calvin. There were also several other Chabochis or outsiders, including one former Tarahumara curer who had left the Sierra to live at a mission near San Francisco de Conchos.

As heavenly hosts, Father Sun and Mother Moon provided their guests with a meal gleaned from the offerings of the Rarámuri, including agave water and tesgüino as well as goat stew, pinole, and tortillas. The guests too honored their hosts with gifts. Ignatius provided all the participants with metal crucifixes, and the salamander passed around several golden plates. Francis, in honor of Mary, Joseph, and the baby Jesus, decorated the eating space with a crèche. Meanwhile, the simple Mennon gave to the others some wheat bread and cheese.

All went well until the guests started to become inebriated from the overconsumption of maize beer. Ignatius no longer attempted to communicate in Rarámuri, lapsing instead into his beloved Latin. Francis clung to his Spanish. Mennon seemed comfortable only in German. The Evangelicals appeared to be speaking in English. And the Pentecostals started speaking in tongues.

Amid the cacophony there arose the specter of anger. The crafty Ignatius accused Francis of ignoring confession and not taking the sacraments often enough. In return, Francis believed Ignatius's arguments were nothing but a holy sham. The salamander was unhappy with the custom of infant baptism as practiced by the Catholic missionaries. Mennon thought that only believers (a category that excluded most Rarámuri) should be baptized and chastised the Catholics for their casual practice of baptizing almost anyone. The Evangelicals viewed the Mennonites as lacking in guilt for the sin of the crucifixion of Christ, while the Pentecostals did not believe anyone, especially their Rarámuri hosts, were true Trinitarians.

From anger came violence, as the bad guests became mean company. Wheat bread, golden plates, and crucifixes were flung across the room. The crèche came tumbling down. Chaos and confusion reigned in the House of the Ones That Walk Above. The souls, nauseated by the smell of tesgüino emanating from the stomachs of the guests, took their leave.

Father Sun and the Annoyer also left in disgust. Both were angered by the Chabochis. From Chínipas they went south to the tranquil Yoquivo. Once again they sat and enjoyed a private communion of goat's blood and maize beer. It was a joyful moment that unfortunately would pass quickly. They knew that the Chabochis would come again and demand another Heavenly Banquet that would once again result in noise, chaos, and violence.

So went the fable of Sisoguichi as told to Naceta, the daughter of a Tepehuán shaman and a Rarámuri peyote doctor. The Sisoguichi legend speaks of the general invasion of Christians throughout the recent history of the Sierra Tarahumara. From the early seventeenth century to the present, a parade of Jesuits, Franciscans, "Josefinos," Mormons, Mennonites, Methodists, Evangelicals, Pentecostals, and others have marched through the mountain and canyonland country. Religious men and their secular allies soon pushed the Tarahumara west and south to the more remote sections of the Sierra.

Yet the Tarahumara survived and persisted. They maintained an indigenous faith that borrowed from Christian ritual those ceremonial elements that reinforced the Rarámuri worldview. While much of the ritual is Christian, the cosmology is predominantly Tarahumara.[1]

The indigenous concept that is probably most widely held by both baptized and nonbaptized Tarahumaras is that of the soul. The Rarámuri think of human beings as bodies with one or more souls; the body, as the souls' house. There is disagreement among the Rarámuri as to the number of souls. Most assume that there are several in every body—large souls in the heart, chest, and brain; smaller ones in the joints, ankles, feet, and other parts of the body. When a person sleeps the soul leaves the body, and the activity of the souls is experienced as dreams. Intoxication occurs when souls, who dislike the smell of beer, leave the body. When a person is ill it is usually because of the abandonment of the body by one or more souls. Serious illnesses occur when a sorcerer bewitches a victim and kidnaps or imprisons the victim's soul. Death is due to the total absence of souls from a person's body.[2]

While gentiles inter their dead in caves, the bautizados, or Christianized Rarámuri, bury their dead in cemeteries located near or in a pueblo. Between death and burial, the body is often left alone inside the dwelling while the women prepare food and the men practice rituals for the death ceremony. After a day or so the body is carried outside and wrapped in a blanket. Agave water is sprinkled over the corpse, and a shaman or religious speaker will instruct the dead not to harm the living. The body is lashed to a pole and carried by the burial party to the burial ground or cemetery. The bearers enter the cemetery, make a counterclockwise turn around the cross erected there, and then make four additional counterclockwise turns around each side of the cross. This symbolizes the arrival of the corpse in the dominion of the dead. The body is then placed in a shallow grave, facing the west, away from the rising sun and the world of the living. The speaker once again implores the deceased to leave the living in peace, and then each person at the grave site drops three (four if the departed is female) pinches of dirt on top of the corpse.[3]

Finally the grave is filled in and the living go back to their homes, never returning to mourn their loved ones. Within three or four years, often in conjunction with Ash Wednesday, a final death rite occurs which involves matachine dancing, musicians, animal sacrifices, drinking of tesgüino, food offerings, and several ritualistic acts, including the crossing of the head with ashes to protect the living from the dead. With this final rite the deceased is believed to have arrived in heaven.[4]

Ideas central to Christianity are absent in Tarahumara thought, for example, the idea of eternal damnation, so dear to fundamentalist Protestants. While Rarámuri souls go to heaven, the Chabochi souls travel to the underworld. If punishment is necessary, the Rarámuri will receive swift and temporary discipline such as scoldings. If the crime is serious, such as murder or incest, the soul will be sent to the Devil for burning. Chabochis are not punished by the Devil, for he is the god of the Chabochis and their misdeeds honor him. The underworld, it should be remembered, while a place of malevolent beings that threaten the Tarahumara, is the heaven of the Chabochi.

The notion of the Holy Trinity is different as well. While Morning Star is often found in association with Father Sun and Mother Moon, forming a kind of divine trilogy, the specific idea of God the Father, the Son, and the Holy Spirit is missing. In Tarahumara sermons, Jesus is never mentioned—only the principal deities, God and God's wife. The sons of the union between God and his wife are called *sukrísto* (from Spanish Jesucristo, Jesus Christ), and the daughters are known as *sánti* (saints). There is also no notion of redemption through Christ's crucifixion. Finally, the Tarahumara, who subscribe to a notion of time that is not only linear but cyclical, lack the strong afterlife orientation of Christians.[5]

Many ideas distinctive to Rarámuri cosmology come from the Tarahumara's religious naturalism. When viewing the sky the Tarahumara see Father Sun and Mother Moon as divine sources of light brightening a path for them to follow. The stars are the souls of small children. Because the soul(s) is likened to breath, wind is considered a being. Whirlwinds are the souls of the dead or souls who leave sleeping bodies. Earthquakes occur when the Devil shakes the columns that support the earth. Plants and animals have souls, and the plant people are found in bulrushes, peyote cacti, and spiny cacti; the Devil's soldiers possess the bodies of coyotes and foxes. Finally, the Rarámuri who leave their homesteads may wander into the *kawichí*, the "wilds" or uncultivated areas of mountains and forests. These are lands outside the moral order, areas of potential evil.[6]

The group that first tended to the Tarahumara souls were known as the Company of Jesus, or the Jesuits, established in 1540 by papal decree. By 1607, when Padre Juan Fonte first made his entrada into Tarahumara country, the Jesuits and their institutions could be found from Prague and Muscovite Russia to the Amazon and the Philippines, from the center of the Catholic world to the peripheries.[7]

Francis Xavier, almost as famous as the Jesuit founder, Ignatius of Loyola, established a mission in Portuguese Goa in 1542 and had reached the Japanese island of Kyushu by 1549. In the 1560s the Jesuits were in Florida and Cuba, and from there, in 1572, they spread their brand of missionary zeal to Mexico City. A decade later they were in Central America, and by 1591 they had inaugurated a mission system among the Indians of northwestern Mexico—a marginal area on the periphery of Spanish rule in Mexico, a colony that was itself a periphery of the Catholic world and the Western global economy.

A century later the Jesuit missions along the river valleys of Sinaloa had sprawled out along the Gulf Coast, crept upward into the Chihuahua Sierra and the deserts of Sonora and Primería Alta (Arizona), and had even crossed the Gulf into Baja California. By the time of their expulsion in the eighteenth century, over three hundred Jesuit missionaries and brothers had served in the Sierra Tarahumara during the previous century and a half, and by 1767 twenty-eight missions administered to the needs of over twenty thousand adult Indians in Upper Tarahumara country.[8]

Tarahumara country was divided into three areas of missionary activity— the Lower Tarahumara, the Upper Tarahumara, and the western section known as Mountain Tarahumara or the Chínipas district (see map 5). The first division was the Misión de la Natividad in the Tarahumara Baja, settled by missionaries and colonists from the Durango area. This area was in the southeastern section of the Sierra Tarahumara, east of the Sierra and part of the Río Conchos watershed.[9]

This district included missions established after 1607 and before 1648. In a report compiled by Padre Juan Ortiz Zapata in 1678, by the third quarter of the seventeenth century the district of the Misión de la Natividad consisted of five *partidos*. A partido was composed of a head mission, or *cabecera* (the term also used by the Spanish to describe a Mexica principal, or head, town in Aztec Mexico) and mission stations, or *pueblos de visitas* (akin to the *sujetos* of provincial Indian Mexico), attached to the head mission, which the missionaries were to visit on a regular basis.[10]

In the Lower Tarahumara were San Miguel de las Bocas south of Parral, San Pablo Ballesa (1611) in the San Pablo valley, San Gerónimo de Huejotitlán (1631) north of the San Pablo mission, and San Felipe de Jesús on the Río Conchos proper. Farther north, on a stream that runs into the Río San Pedro (which in turn drains into the Conchos), the mission church of San Francisco Xavier de Satevó was constructed in 1648 (map 5).[11]

By the early 1700s, these missions were combined with the Zona Tepehuán to form a single province, and then in 1753 this province was transferred from Jesuit administration to the secular clergy and the bishop of Durango. Secularization facilitated the settlement of lands that had previously belonged to the Jesuit community or the Tarahumara. This region, close to Spanish towns and mining camps, attracted a mix of peoples, including several tribal Indians from central Mexico as well as blacks and mulattoes. It was more like the Franciscan world of eastern Nueva Vizcaya or the greater Parral area then the Sierra Tarahumara. The Lower Tarahumara was the only area of Jesuit activity where the reducción was partially successful, resulting in today's acculturated Tarahumaras who have lost their Rarámuri identity.[12]

In the Upper Tarahumara were the missions of San Joaquín and Santa Ana. This area was composed of missions that, although established earlier, had been destroyed in the rebellions of 1648, 1650, and 1652 and reestablished after 1673. Again, according to Father Juan, by the end of the seventeenth century this region contained nine partidos consisting of nine cabeceras and thirty-seven visitas. One of the earliest missions was San Francisco de Borja, upriver from San Francisco Xavier de Satevó near the headwaters of the Río San Pedro.[13]

In the 1670s several missions were reestablished, including Nonoava, Carichí, and Sisoguichi, the first on the Conchos proper, the latter two on the headwaters of the Conchos. Neighboring Bocoyna (1702) and Cusárare (1740) were settled later. At the headwaters of the Urique was the cabecera mission of Norogachi. In 1673, fifteen years prior to the discovery of silver north of the Laguna de los Mexicanos, San Bernabé Cusihuíriachi was founded. Again in the 1670s, in the far northwestern section of the Tarahumara Alta along the Río Papigochi, several missions were developed including Papigochi, Temósachi, and in the far north, Yepómera. West of the Río Papigochi, near Pima country and the northwestern edge of the Upper Tarahumara, were Tomochi and Tutuaca (map 5).[14]

The third district of the Sierra Tarahumara contained missions that had been established west of the Tarahumara Alta. The earliest were located in the mountain area of Chínipas; the later ones, in the hot canyonlands of the Urique, Batopilas, and Verde rivers. Whereas the Lower and Upper Tarahumara had been settled mostly from the Durango region, the Chínipas district was established by explorers and missionaries from Sinaloa.

The first entry into the country of the Chínipas Indians came in 1589 when the governor of Nueva Vizcaya sent several military men and colonists from Culiacán to the mountain country west of the Tarahumara Alta. The Portuguese Jesuit, Pedro Mendes, followed up this expedition with his own entrada in 1601, where he made his first contact with the Tarahumara.[15]

The initial founding of the Chínipas mission was delayed by Indian resistance until 1626. Further rebellions a decade later by neighboring Guazapares led to the abandonment of the region, with many Christianized Tarahumaras traveling to the Sinaloa missions beyond the Sierra Tarahumara. It was not until 1676 that Chínipas was reestablished.[16]

From Chínipas, Jesuit influence spread north to the headwaters of the Mayo River where missionaries at Morís (1690) attended to the needs of the Varohio Indians; southeast along the Río Verde where the Baborigame and Nabogame missions (1670s) were organized in the Zona Tepehuán; and east, following the Fuerte upriver from Sinaloa, in the land of the Tubares, Temores, and Guazapares along the Septentrión and Fuerte rivers (1670–1700s).

In 1680, the Italian padre, Gian Maria Salvatierra (the same missionary who later established missions in Baja California), left the Temores and Guazapares and traveled up the Septentrión to Cuiteco. At a point overlooking Urique Canyon he colonized the mission of San Francisco Xavier de Cerocahui (originally Selógachi). From here visitations were made to Tarahumara homesteads near Cuiteco and Satevó (on the Batopilas River), as well as to pueblos of the Guazapares and Tubares. Cerocahui was also the departure point for settlements across Urique Canyon, including the Pamáchi area (and, later, Samachique).[17]

Meanwhile miners from Sonora discovered mineral wealth in Los Alamos (1686), and subsequently the silver camp of Cusihuíriachi was established (1687). Three years later a Spaniard named Juan Vallejo, corroborating information obtained from a Tarahumara informant, uncovered a wealthy silver vein in Urique (below Cerocahui on the Río Urique).[18]

An influx of miners soon led to other discoveries in the Chínipas district, including, between 1711 and 1720, the rich silver deposits of Batopilas (on the river of the same name). Its importance was highlighted in 1732 when the *alcaldía mayor* (central municipality), originally located in Urique, was transferred to Batopilas. By 1734 all of the missions in the mountains and canyonlands west of the Tarahumara Alta were organized into the Chínipas mission province, and by midcentury there were twelve cabeceras in the Chínipas district.[19]

Three miles downriver from the town of Batopilas, Santo Angel Custodio de Satevó, founded in 1699, was still a visita of Tubares in 1739. After 1740 a mission church was started. Originally built by the Jesuits, it was later rebuilt by the Franciscans. The first missionaries came from the partido of Concepción de los Tubares, with visitas that served the Tubar Indians who lived in the triangular area where the Batopilas River joins the Sinforosa Canyon. The same missionaries who baptized and administered the sacraments to the Tubares were now expected to work simultaneously with the Tarahumaras of Satevó. The languages were as different as night and day. Not only were there linguistic hurdles but the Satevó area was a hostile and difficult environment and the Tarahumaras here were unfriendly gentiles who were related to others who had earlier abandoned the faith.[20]

Even today the remains of the Satevó church are magnificent to view. Standing alone on the edge of the Batopilas River, the majesty and dignity of the place is a memorial to the Jesuits and their Christian faith. A popular guidebook by Richard D. Fisher refers to it as the "Lost Cathedral," "deep in the Grand Canyon of Mexico, unaccounted for, shrouded in mystery and legend." Although it was not lost then (especially to the natives of the Sierra) and was a church and not a cathedral, Fisher's description is a testimony to the magical and mystical quality of this spectacular and rugged area.[21]

The size of the church is perhaps its most notable feature. Although the area is isolated today, it is obvious that a large Tarahumara labor force had to be assembled to build it. It is very likely that there were many more Tarahumaras in the area in the eighteenth century than today, and if not native to the area, they were brought in originally to work the various silver veins that were found throughout the desert valley.

Under the supervision of the Jesuits, the Tarahumara molded thousands of clay bricks that were hardened on the spot, and, with calcium deposits from the silver veins and sand from the riverbed, a durable type of lime-and-sand mortar was made. The roof has three domes—one large, one medium, and one small on top of the bell tower—and four half-domes. It also has a vaulted ceiling. The gem of the Satevó church is its bell tower (very likely a post-Jesuit addition that had four small and four medium bells with a large bell in the center—only four of which remained as of 1990). The original bells were cast in the area. A library whose shelves were once filled with parchment tomes is on one side of the high altar. A connecting door through the library opens out onto an adobe monastery (long since eroded) that contained a fruit tree and flower garden. In the land of gold and silver, the church at Satevó was and is a special treasure.[22]

Satevó, like many of the missions of the Sierra, was converted to a Franciscan center after the Jesuit expulsion of 1767. Initially, in 1767, it was annexed to the beneficiary at Batopilas, which was in turn controlled from the diocese in Durango. In 1793 it was transferred from the secular parish of Batopilas to the Franciscans. At the end of the century, as a *misión cabecera*, it had attached to it the visitas of Yoquivo, Guadalupe, and Guapaleina. Although it was listed on the church rolls in 1803, it was not registered in 1812. Throughout the nineteenth century it was largely ignored, first by the Franciscans and later by the secular church authorities. Very likely, in the absence of the priests, the Tarahumaras conducted their somewhat syncretic services themselves.[23]

As can be seen even today, the Jesuits in the colonial period met with limited success in converting the Rarámuri to Christianity. Very early in the seventeenth century the Tarahumara developed what Merrill describes as a "counterideology" that portrayed the priests as Spanish sorcerers and associated baptism and church bells with disease, death, and sterile land. The Indians soon learned that those Tarahumaras who went to the missions seldom returned to their homesteads. If they did not weaken and die from exploitation on farms and mines, they would die from European diseases.[24]

In addition, in the Upper Tarahumara and Chínipas districts, permanent congregation of people in mission villages was impractical because fertile plots were small and scattered. The Tarahumara preferred to stay at their isolated homesteads to raise their crops and protect their fields from pests and livestock. Although the Tarahumara readily took to the Easter and Christmas ceremonies staged at the church, the Jesuits constantly complained that the Tarahumara could not receive the Eucharist because they could not conceive of the idea of God hidden in the Host. Ultimately, the Tarahumara's favorable response to the Catholic rituals did not extend to tutelage in formal Catholic canon.[25]

In surveying the entire Sierra Tarahumara, it appears that Catholic instruction and Spanish assimilation were stronger in the Tarahumara Baja than elsewhere. In the Tarahumara Alta and the Chínipas area, the Tarahumara, while rejecting the idea of Jesuit congregations, did adopt some institutions and idioms. But there is diversity even here, with, for example, Sisoguichi, a Catholic headquarters and apostolic vicariate with a clinic and boarding school, having more Christianized Indians today than do outlying pueblos like Samachique or Aboreáchi. Tarahumara identity is more intact, of course, among those gentiles who inhabit the more remote reaches of Tarahumara country that the Jesuits did not contact until the mid-eighteenth century. It is not surprising, then, that in the Sierra Tarahumara, Judas figures symbolize fertility and the evil influence of Chabochis more often than they do the betrayal of Christ.[26]

In 1767, Charles III, motivated as much by political as religious concerns, expelled the Company of Jesus from the possessions of the Spanish Empire. The expulsion order affected all of New Spain, and in July the governor of Nueva Vizcaya rounded up nineteen Jesuit missionaries from the Tarahumara Alta and sent them to waiting ships in the harbor of Veracruz. The order did not affect the Tarahumara Baja since it had been secularized earlier.

In 1767 there were at least twenty-eight Jesuit missions and possibly as many as fifty-five visitas in Tarahumara country. While twelve were secularized and placed under the authority of the bishop, most of the others came under the control of Franciscan fathers from the college of Nuestra Señora de Guadalupe in Zacatecas (independent monastic schools that had been missionizing the Texas and Nuevo Santander areas). Although the Franciscans confronted many of the same problems with the Tarahumara that had earlier faced the Jesuits (e.g., tesgüino drinking, abandonment of mission pueblos, shamanism), the documentation suggests that at the end of the eighteenth century there was more a continuation than a disruption of Jesuit policies. By the beginning of the nineteenth century, the Franciscans were administrating eleven cabeceras and twenty-three visitas in the Chínipas district alone.[27]

Since the bulk of Franciscan efforts in Nueva Vizcaya were in the Conchería (the homeland of the Concho Indians in the lowlands east of the Sierra Tarahumara) in the area of Spanish settlement, their missionary activity could not proceed without interference from other segments of Spanish society. This proximity to non-Indian communities, along with the presence of a variety of Indian groups, meant that a stable atmosphere was lacking which could aid the instruction of neophytes. The Franciscans were often either unable to learn the language of any particular indigenous group or unwilling to study the vernacular. Like some Jesuits, they had to use Spanish to communicate with their various charges.[28]

The Franciscan effort was hindered by the arrival of several non-Conchos refugees to the Conchería and their missions during the first seventy years of the eighteenth century. As Tobosos and Conchos died off or left the Conchería, they were replaced by Tarahumaras. The Rarámuri fled the Jesuit missions of Satevó, San Francisco de Borja, Carichí, and other settlements on the upper San Pedro River and went east to join raiding bands on the Chihuahua plains. The membership of these bands included individuals of mixed Indian, African, and European ancestry.[29]

Others came to the Conchería against their will, the results of labor repartimientos in mines and haciendas or forced congregation in the Franciscan missions. Some Franciscan missions on the edge of the Sierra Tarahumara, such as Babonoyaba on the San Pedro River and Namiquipa north of Papigochi, that were inhabited by Conchos in the seventeenth century had become Tarahumaran by the end of the eighteenth.[30]

By the beginning of the national era (around 1830), the disintegration of the Tarahumara missions was obvious. Having limited resources, the Franciscans could not attend to all the needs of the Sierra Tarahumara, and many of the secularized missions were unable to maintain resident priests. Although ten missions remained in the Sierra Tarahumara until 1854, most of the missions were ignored and eventually abandoned, with the possible exception of Cerocahui. Here the Franciscans did manage to construct a beautiful stone carved altar, and people in the area still sing songs and repeat litanies that are of Franciscan origin. In Cerocahui, unlike the other Franciscan missions, the missionaries did attempt to learn the Rarámuri language. In addition, west of Cerocahui beyond the Urique and Cobre canyons, the Franciscans established a new mission church in Basíhuare, a visita of Cusárare, after 1825.[31]

In spite of these small gains, the Franciscans were even less successful than the Jesuits in indoctrinating the Tarahumara in their missions, and by 1859 all of the Franciscan missions in Mexico were secularized. Those in the Sierra were first under the authority of the bishop of Durango and after 1891 the bishop of Chihuahua. In the 1890s, Lumholtz reported that in Norogachi he found "the residence of the only priest living in the Tarahumare country."[32]

The Jesuits returned to Chihuahua and the Sierra Tarahumara in 1900. In a few years they had reestablished missions in Norogachi, Tónachi (outside of Guachochi today), Jesús María (near Morís and Ocampo in the northwestern part of the Sierra Tarahumara), Carichí, Nonoava, and Sisoguichi.[33]

The reestablishment of the missions was temporarily halted in July 1914. Francisco (Pancho) Villa was then the most important revolutionary leader in Chihuahua. Thinking the missionaries were supporters of his enemy, Venustiano Carranza, Villa deported all foreign Jesuits to the United States. A few years later, between 1925 and 1929, several Jesuits were caught in the web of Plutarco Calles's war on the church and were expelled from the Sierra and imprisoned. Conditions-improved only after Lázaro Cárdenas come to power in 1934.[34]

In 1938 the padre Andrés Lira, with an enthusiasm matching that of his seventeenth-century brothers, remodeled the church at Cerocahui (he built a new tower and made the church one of the showpieces of Chihuahua), established a boarding school, and started a medical dispensary. By 1946 the Jesuits were once again well entrenched in the Sierra, with eleven fathers, six scholastics, and seven brothers working in six centers (Sisoguichi, Norogachi, Narárachi, Chinatu, Guadalupe y Clavo, and, of course, Cerocahui). In that year the Jesuits estimated that of the 40,000 Tarahumaras in the Sierra, only 5,000 were gentiles, and they lived mostly in the canyons around Cusárare and the rancherías between Samachique and Yoquivo. Nearly 13,000 of the 40,000 Tarahumaras spoke only Tarahumar and knew no Spanish.[35]

In the early 1950s, reflecting the compliant voice of Pope Pius XII who spoke of planting the seeds of the gospel in a variety of patches, the Jesuits inaugurated a program to enhance communication within the mission system and extend their activities to the gentiles. This new gospel allowed a more flexible religion to be practiced, one that incorporated folk practices and beliefs into traditional Catholicism. Using shortwave radios, pickup trucks, and small aircraft, the Jesuits expanded the range and effectiveness of their mission. By the 1980s most Tarahumaras, including the gentiles, had been baptized.[36]

Until 1994 the Jesuit mission had as its headquarters for the entire Sierra Tarahumara the apostolic vicariate of Sisoguichi, a mission town with a long historical tradition that has become a hub of missionary activity. Its vicar serves as a titular bishop representing the bishop and the pope in ecclesiastical matters. In addition, Sisoguichi is the home of a large boarding school, a hospital with an operating room, a pharmacy, a treatment clinic, and several carpenter and machine shops. Parish headquarters are in Cerocahui, Norogachi, and Creel. Of the thirty-eight clerics in the Sierra, about half are diocesan priests and half are Jesuits. Not all mission churches have a permanent ordained pastor who can offer the sacraments each Sunday.[37]

Father Luis Verplancken, who reflects the spirit of the Jesuits' new program, is one of Creel's greatest assets. Father Luis came to the area in 1952 and was in charge of a boarding school. He then left the Sierra for Mexico City, where he studied theology, and then Louisiana, to learn about agriculture. In 1960 he returned, first to Sisoguichi and then as pastor of the Creel parish, an area that included fifteen thousand people and the visitas of San Ignacio, Cusárare, Basíhuare, Samachique, and Choguita. In addition, there was a school to administer in Rejogochi.[38]

On discovering an infant mortality rate of over 80 percent, he attempted to serve the Indians by traveling in his four-wheel-drive Scout throughout the Sierra. The enemy was malnutrition, scurvy, dysentery, pneumonia, polio, and especially tuberculosis (a never-ending struggle as there was a fivefold increase of the disease in the greater Creel area between 1986 and 1991). By 1965, with the help of volunteers and donations, he had started a small hospital in an old railroad warehouse in Creel. A major need was clear running water, so Father Luis initiated a project that soon resulted in a four-mile pipeline with three handcrafted pumping stations that brought water to Creel.[39]

By 1979, again with the help of volunteers under Father Luis's guidance, a seventy-one-bed hospital, the Clínica de Santa Teresita (named for the patroness of the missions) was completed which today services 12,000 to 13,000 people with its laboratory, dental care unit, X-ray equipment, surgery room, pharmacy, and kitchen. By 1992, to stop the scourge of tuberculosis and complement the activities of the clinic, an outreach program in preventive medicine has been initiated which utilizes the talents of trained health promotores (mostly Tarahumara women). Finally, visiting medical professionals arrive periodically via the St. Jude Express (a small aviation service out of Albuquerque) bearing supplies and precious skills.[40]

The Jesuits also have an educational plan for the Sierra. Their boarding schools teach the Rarámuri youth Spanish, Indian crafts, hygiene, and irrigation and farming methods. Father Luis is also the initiator of the Indian craft shop in Creel. At the schools, the Tarahumara learn new skills for weaving blankets, carving wooden animals, making clay pots, and creating miniature dolls. Most of these items are not indigenous to the Tarahumara. The crafts are then sold in the Jesuit store in Creel to tourists, and the profits help to support the clinic. The entire operation is run primarily from private contributions with some governmental assistance.[41]

Although the Jesuits are the dominant influence in the Sierra Tarahumara, some non-Catholic groups have been in the Sierra since the late nineteenth century. Between 1875 and 1876, Brigham Young, president of the Church of Jesus Christ of Latter-Day Saints, more commonly known as the Mormons, sponsored an exploratory and proselytizing journey to Mexico. Their mission was to look for places to colonize (especially if the church in Utah was forced to resettle because of the hostility of the federal government over the issue of polygamy) and to teach the gospel to the Indians.[42]

A small group of Mormons traveled on horseback through Phoenix and Tucson to El Paso del Norte on the Río Grande. From El Paso they went to Chihuahua City. They were not well received in either El Paso or Chihuahua City. Unhappy with their lack of success in the cities, the missionary party, having heard that there were many Indians in the mountains, turned west and traveled to the rural community of Guerrero in the Sierra Madre foothills.[43]

It was here, on the edge of the Sierra Tarahumara, that the group met with its first real success. There was no clerical opposition, the people were not devout Catholics, and the municipal authorities granted them permission to preach. From Guerrero they took their message to the Tarahumaras, first in Arísiachi and later in Mátachi and Temósachi in the Papigochi Valley. These Tarahumaras were very friendly to the missionaries and were impressed by the Mormon promise that the Rarámuri, as Lamanites, would have a special role to perform at the end of the millennial era as the builders of the temple at New Jerusalem, a city on the American continent that would be, like its ancient counterpart, a holy city, a Zion, a city of God. When the Mormons left the Sierra Tarahumara, the Rarámuri provided them with so much corn and beans that their pack animals were overloaded.[44]

Leaving Tarahumara country behind, the party traveled north along the Casas Grande River and eventually returned to New Mexico and the United States. Their explorations along the Casas Grande and its tributaries soon led to the establishment of several Mormon colonies in the area, including Colonia Díaz (1887), Colonia Juárez (1887), Colonia Dublán (1888), and, in high country at over 7,000 feet, Colonia García (1898). In 1889 with the church near bankruptcy and its leaders in hiding, the Mexican mission was closed and foreign missionaries were withdrawn. The Mexican branches were left to their own devices for a thirteen-year period.[45]

Finally, in 1901, the church returned, only to be forced out again in 1912 when the Mexican Revolution arrived in the person of General José Inés Salazar who ordered Junius Romney, president of the Juárez stake, and the Mormons to surrender their firearms, leave their colonies, and join in a modern-day exodus to El Paso. In November 1917 the Mormons received permission to return to Mexico, and by the 1920s the colonies had been reestablished. Although only Mexican citizens were allowed to proselytize, in 1938 the church had twenty-six young men from the colonies acting as missionaries in Mexico.[46]

In the early 1990s Mexico was divided into 126 Mormon stakes (each stake has several wardhouses or church buildings) and a variety of mission areas that included several stakes. The state of Chihuahua was divided into twelve mission zones, each under the jurisdiction of the mission president in Chihuahua City. The Sierra Tarahumara is one mission zone, and in 1990 it had fourteen Mormon missionaries—thirteen Mexicans and one gringo. They supposedly carried the message to both Mexicans and Tarahumaras, although no missionaries spoke Tarahumar. In the previous year they had performed nineteen baptisms in Creel (a banner year for Catholics as well that included a trip by the pope to Mexico).[47]

Another non-Catholic group that has made small inroads into the Sierra Tarahumara are the Mennonites. Most are descendants of the conservative Old Colony that left Manitoba and Saskatchewan in Canada between 1921 and 1927 to settle in Mexico, especially Chihuahua.[48] Many Mennonites settled close to the city of Cuauhtémoc, approximately sixty miles west of Chihuahua City and ninety miles northeast of Creel. In the 1990s this area was the home of about 32,000 Mennonites who lived in more than one hundred fifty villages and camps around Cuauhtémoc. The Mennonites are the leading oat producers in Mexico, and their cheeses and cured meats are esteemed throughout the country. They are also the largest producers of apples in Chihuahua.[49]

Many Mennonites, like those who live in the Swift Current Colony north of Cuauhtémoc, promote a more progressive lifestyle than that of the fundamentalist Old Colony. Their men generally dress in Western attire akin to middle-class Mexicans in the area. Their church building is large and imposing. They drive motor vehicles and use farm equipment and tractors with rubber tires.

In contrast to the "progressives" are the Old Colony Mennonites of Colonia Capulín and other colonies in the far northwestern part of the state, midway between Nuevo Casas Grandes and Palomas. These "fundamentalists" use horse-drawn buggies, dress in traditional style (men in denim overalls and straw hats; women with typical Mennonite headgear and attire with subdued colors), have austere dwellings and buildings, and operate a monolingual education program in German. Most Mennonites, progressive or not, unlike the Mormons, do not proselytize, preferring to withdraw from the larger community so as to preserve their special ways and mores, a way of life that opposes military service and secular education.[50]

From time to time the Mennonite camps near Cuauhtémoc would send individuals into the Sierra on missions of mercy. In the early 1980s, when many Tarahumaras were suffering from malnutrition, the Mennonites brought several truckloads of food into the country. One of these individuals, Pedro Martin, was a Mennonite representative who brought cheese, corn, flour, and beans to Creel and Batopilas to feed the Indians.[51] He first came into the Sierra to instruct the Rarámuri of San Ignacio how to operate and service a tractor and eventually established a small rancho a Humirá, on the edge of Copper Canyon. Here Pedro and his wife, Helen grew fruit trees and raised corn and beans. They hoped to be an example to their Tarahumara neighbors and show that discipline and hard work would bring spiritual and material rewards. As Pedro said, "It's better to show them how to fish, then simply give them fish. That is God's way." However, God's way was not everlasting and the Martins were eventually forced to forsake their Sierra haven and return to the camps at Cuauhtémoc.[52]

The twentieth century has seen the arrival of a number of Protestant groups in the Sierra Tarahumara. During the 1920s the Methodists initiated a ministry in Bocoyna and, with assistance from members in El Paso, planned a Protestant University there. Methodism spread from Bocoyna to San Juanito, Creel, and even the Tarahumara area of Choguita.[53]

In the 1940s an Evangelical group entered Samachique when the Catholics temporarily abandoned it. And more recently, in 1990, a nondenominational Pentecostal assembly gathered in Creel from Lyndale, Texas, to establish a three-year ministry. Their tent city consisted of an office, homes, a clinic, and a cross-cultural training center that would bring the gospel to the Tarahumara. Not successful in buying land in Creel, they were forced by the local authorities to leave the following year.[54]

In fact, the Sierra, dominated by Catholic mestizos and quasi-Christianized, indigenous heathens, is not always friendly to Protestant outsiders. At Panalachi in late May 1990, I saw a small store with the following sign in the window:

Por favor no toque
Este hogar es católico.
No aceptamos propaganda protestante
Ni testigos de Jehova
y de ninguna otra secta.

Please do not knock or call
This is a Catholic place.
We do not accept either Protestant propaganda
or that of Jehovah's Witnesses
or any other sect.

At least the *evangelistas,* the name most Mexicans use for all Protestants, were not targeted for murder—a fate that has befallen more than one individual in the remote villages of Mexico where the people protect their own brand of folk Catholicism with religious fervor, fanaticism, and, at times, violence.[55]

The history of religion in the Sierra Tarahumara reflects many of the national and international trends. The Mexicans, Tarahumara or mestizo, are a ritual people. The Rarámuri, borrowing from Jesuit teachings, incorporated Catholic ceremonies and Christian dramas into their religious cosmology. When the Jesuits were expelled and Franciscan resources ran low, the missions were mostly ignored. In the nineteenth century, when Apache attacks and Mexican colonization drove the Tarahumara deeper into the mountains and canyons, their increased isolation meant that, with no priests to catechize them, they were free to shape their own native religious traditions.

Although the Jesuits returned after 1900, by the 1950s their goals had changed. No longer was religious conversion of the Tarahumara the most important consideration. Their welfare and, for the Mexican state, their incorporation into the Mexican Republic were the important objectives. Under the umbrella of ecumenism, both the Catholic church and the Mexican state became more tolerant.

In the meantime, evangelistas, aided indirectly by the anticlericalism of the

Mexican government, continued to quote the Bible, search for souls, and warn the people of idolatry. Through it all, most Tarahumaras have had little time or inclination to listen to outsiders. They are preoccupied with the care of their Rarámuri souls.

The Sierra Christ, Creel, 1989

Mission church, San Ignacio, 1989

Visiting the Christian god, San Ignacio, 1992

Matachine dancers, near Cusárare, 1992

Epiphany, near Cusárare, 1992

Resting place of the souls, San Ignacio, 1989

Tarahumara youth in the kawichí, 1992

Above: Santo Angel Custodio de Satevó, 1990

Below: Dome, Satevó mission church, 1990

96

Bell tower and dome, Satevó, 1990

Church bell, Satevó, 1990

Interior, Satevó mission church, 1990

Church bell, La Bufa mining town, 1990

Above: Virgin of Guadalupe, church interior, Bufa, 1990

Below: Sukrísto, Batopilas, 1990

Father Luis and communicants, San Ignacio, 1992

Church, Creel, 1988

Martin MacIntyre, volunteer doctor from Scotland, Creel clinic, 1989

Dennis (West Jordan, Utah) and Carlos (Sonora),
Mormon missionaries, Creel, 1990

Helen Martin and husband Pedro, Humirá, 1990

Pentecostal, Creel, 1990

Road to Batopilas, 1992

Remnant from "caravan of beasts," Batopilas, 1989

Batopilas plaza, 1990

Eulalio Bustillos and his wedding picture, Batopilas, 1989

Department of Sanitation, Batopilas, 1990

Shepherd's castle, Batopilas, 1989

La Hacienda San Miguel, Batopilas, 1989

Porfirio Díaz Tunnel, Batopilas, 1990

Looking out over Tomochi from cave, 1989

Entry to mine shaft, La Bufa, 1990

Hydroelectricity, Batopilas, 1990

Slaughter at Batopilas, 1990

At home, near the road between La Bufa and Batopilas, 1990

CHAPTER FOUR

THE SEARCH FOR EL DORADO

Of all the States of the Mexican Republic, Chihuahua is, without contradiction, the richest in minerals, and we count no less than three thousand different leads, the greater part of which are silver.

Roger Dubois, French Consul, 1864 Report

THE BUS RIDE from Creel to Batopilas takes the better part of a day. It is an eighty-four mile, 6,000-foot descent over dirt roads, across arroyos and barrancas, into Batopilas Canyon. There, at 1,650 feet, nestled along the banks of the Río Batopilas, is the old silver mining town of Batopilas. Greeting travelers on their arrival in Batopilas are the ruins of Shepherd's Castle, a Gothic revival structure at the entrance to the Hacienda San Miguel that dominates the town and adds to its reputation as a historic mining center. Batopilas was and is famed in international mining circles for its native silver. And it was mining of precious minerals that was the engine of the Spanish Empire in America—silver in Potosí (Peru) and New Spain (colonial Mexico), gold in Colombia.

In the half century after the discovery of silver in Potosí in 1545, the amount of gold and silver in Europe tripled, with America's output of precious metals being ten times greater than that of the rest of the world. In 1546, Juan de Tolosa discovered a silver bonanza among the *chichimeca* people of Zacatecas. He named the mine La Bufa. A few years later the mines of Guanajuato and Taxco were opened. At the same time ore was discovered at Santa Bárbara, the first such find in the present state of Chihuahua. Then came Parral, Urique, Cusihuíriachi, Chínipas, and Santa Eulalia—all in Nueva Vizcaya. By the 1740s, the deepest mountain penetration yet, the area of Batopilas, began to boom.[1]

By 1750, Mexico was the wealthiest colony of Spain's American empire, with Mexican and American silver making possible a global economy. By the end of the eighteenth century, the most productive mines were those of Guanajuato, Catorce, and Zacatecas. In addition, the famous German mining engineer, Baron Alexander von Humboldt, ranked Taxco eighth and Batopilas ninth in his ordering of the richest mines of New Spain. Mexico provided Spain with the lion's share of silver coins and ingots then in circulation.[2]

Some of the silver reached Europe through contraband dealings with the Dutch and English enemies of Spain. More of it was traded by Spain's foreign merchants—Genoese, French, Dutch, and English—to the Ottomans, Chinese, and East Indians.[3] Almost all the silver in circulation in the Far East at this time came either directly across the Pacific from Acapulco to Manila in the Philippines or from Europe by way of Mexico and Peru. The historian Fernand Braudel noted that based on official figures for 1785, "Latin America was sending back to Europe every year four or five times as much as India. This would certainly make it the greatest treasure-store in the world."[4]

Parral and Urique were important mines in the seventeenth century. The *reales de minas* (royal mines) of Batopilas, although discovered in the early eighteenth century, did not become a famous bonanza until after 1740, and the boom lasted until the Mexican independence movement of 1810. During these years the population of Batopilas grew to 11,000 inhabitants—10,000 of whom were classified as "Indians." Tarahumaras and mules were used for transport purposes: the Tarahumaras lifted heavy loads of ore in leather buckets up steep wooden ladders; mules were used to turn windlasses or as "caravans of beasts" to move silver coins and ingots to Mexico City. Over time the colonial city began to reveal its wealth as streets were paved with silver bars and common miners were transformed into grand dukes.[5]

Batopilas was also the alcaldía mayor of a district (known as a partido; not to be confused with mission areas of the same name) that spread from today's northwestern Durango to Sinaloa and the Río Chínipas in the west. This district, one of twenty-two in the province of Nueva Vizcaya in 1786, included the silver mining community of Urique and the wealthy gold camps of Cerro Colorado and Satevó. The governor, as the viceroy's representative in the province, dealt directly with the alcalde mayor of each partido. It was his responsibility to see that the royal mining taxes, licenses, and monopolies were enforced.[6]

According to a royal decree of 1790, the commission of the Royal Tribunal of Mines reported that from the Batopilas district there was extracted within a few years over $50 million worth of silver. This official figure did not include silver surreptitiously taken by miners attempting to avoid royal taxes. Assuming that at least one-fifth of the total went to the Crown as taxes (the *quinta real*), it would mean that the king of Spain obtained more than $10 million from the Batopilas area alone during the late eighteenth century.[7]

The wars of independence and their aftermath led to a decline of the mining industry of Mexico. Mines were flooded, haciendas were scorched, capital took flight with the Spaniards, and people abandoned their farms. In Batopilas downpours deluged the trails and collapsed buildings. Depopulation left the town with only ten resident families in 1845. A revival did occur, though, when local and foreign entrepreneurs initiated a recovery after 1852. Old mines were reopened and new ones begun. During the resurgence period, the San Antonio, a mine that had been worked earlier by Mexicans, was purchased in 1861 by Wells, Fargo & Company, and in 1879, Wells, Fargo sold its rights to an American investor from Washington, D.C., Alexander Robey Shepherd. This signaled a new phase in the history of Batopilas and the mining industry of Mexico.[8]

To understand what drove Shepherd to leave Washington, D.C., in 1879 for Batopilas, one has to appreciate its colonial heritage and its reputation for silver bonanzas right up to the end of the nineteenth century. Shepherd's contemporary, Frederick Schwatka, wrote in the early 1890s that if you took Batopilas as a base and drew from that base a radius of two hundred miles, that is, a diameter of four hundred miles from the center of Batopilas, "there is no doubt that the resulting circle will include the richest mining district in America, and probably the world. . . . From within that circle comes a little over one-fourth the bullion of the whole of Mexico." In addition, Shepherd was well aware of the many references to Batopilas in the works of Baron von Humboldt. Batopilas appeared to be an overripe plum begging to be picked.[9]

Shepherd was born in Washington, D.C., on 31 January 1835, the son of a businessman. During his lifetime the industrial revolution would come to America. In 1835 the United States had little more than 1,000 miles of railroad track in use. Before his thirteenth birthday, James W. Marshall discovered some gold nuggets along the American River, and a year later the gold rush was on. When Shepherd died in 1902, the United States had more than 200,000 miles of track, and this increased to 250,000 by the start of the Mexican Revolution of 1910. A year before his death, in 1901, word would come to Batopilas about the discovery of "black gold" near Port Arthur, Texas. Between the discovery of gold in California and oil in Texas, the society of the trans-Mississippi West, including that part of the Greater Southwest that contained Batopilas, would be transformed from one of subsistence agriculture to that of a modernized and urbanized capitalistic economy integrated into a global structure.[10]

Shepherd, the man who loved precious metals, especially gold (yellow and black) and silver, brought the industrial revolution to Batopilas. He ushered in the modern phase of its mining history—a history characterized by the new capital-intensive mining machinery, financial mechanisms, and techniques of the industrial revolution. He was the Gilded Age's representative to Mexico, the ultimate capitalist in the Age of Capital.

For several years after the Civil War, Shepherd served in public office, an involvement that eventually brought him influence and contacts in the politics of the city of Washington, D.C. In 1871 he became vice president of the Board of Public Works with responsibility for developing the city's walkways, roads, and sewers as well as for generally beautifying the capital. While many of these responsibilities were met, Shepherd and the board were constantly facing problems of overspending and cost overruns. Allegations of fraud and embezzlement soon led to congressional investigations of Shepherd and the members of the board as well as President Ulysses S. Grant. As quickly as Grant appointed Shepherd territorial governor of Washington, D.C. (13 September 1873), Congress abolished the territorial form of government (20 June 1874).[11]

Having fallen from power, in financial straits, and out of luck, Shepherd was casting about for some way to recoup his losses outside Washington. And the American owners of the Batopilas mines were looking for a buyer. His one-way ticket out of the political capital of Washington would take him to the silver bonanza capital of the world.

In 1879 his entourage left Washington, D.C., for Mexico, via Panama to Mazatlán. From there they took a schooner to Agiabampo, on the Gulf of California, where the party formed a mule train for Batopilas. After riding several days in the boiling sun, they arrived in the promised land. The potential for profit was great. Pleased with what he saw, Shepherd bought up several mining interests and returned immediately to Washington to gather his family and set up business in Batopilas. In New York he organized the Consolidated Batopilas Mining Company and purchased the properties of William G. Fargo and his associates, taking them into his board of directors.

That next year Shepherd, accompanied by his wife, seven children, and four dogs, took the train to San Antonio, Texas. From there, the end of the rail line in 1880, they hired wagons to take them to Chihuahua, being escorted through Fort Concho and Fort Davis by the U.S. Army. Finally, after nearly six months of travel, they arrived in Batopilas.

Soon after reaching the region, Shepherd began to develop his company's mining properties and to enlarge his holdings. By 1887 the new enterprises were consolidated into the Batopilas Mining Company, a corporation that took over the operations of seven major mining firms. New purchases were covered by a $1 million, 6 percent gold bond, with the Knickerbocker Trust Company of New York holding the mortgage and securing the loan.[12]

It was the financial failure of this trust in 1909 that caused the Batopilas Mining Company much stress. When the Mexican Revolution erupted the next year, disruptions along the supply route made it almost impossible to continue operation. After 1914 most of Shepherd's American employees returned to the United States. Silver production between 1911 and 1920 was less than one-fourth of that for the preceding decade. After 1926 the bondholders and shareholders gave up all efforts to keep the mines operating.[13]

During the late nineteenth century, what is known as the Porfiriato in Mexican history, Shepherd's Castle and the mining complex associated with it, together known as the Hacienda San Miguel, dominated the town of Batopilas. While the hacienda was located on the east bank of the river, most of the town (of what became 5,000 individuals in Shepherd's time) was along the west bank and ran south along the river. San Miguel was the center of Shepherd's operations as well as his living quarters.

Although some historians insist that the three-story masonry "castle" served as the Shepherd family residence, Grant Shepherd, one of Alexander's sons, indicated that the structure was an office building. The historian David Pletcher insists that the family occupied a modest one-story adobe building, little different from any middle-class home in Don Porfirio's Mexico. It was equipped with certain unlikely comforts, however, among them an ice machine and a grand piano that had been packed in on the backs of Tarahumaras. Shepherd also built a second house in the mountains as a retreat from the hot weather.[14]

The image of Shepherd as a kind of feudal baron living in ostentatious fashion and ruling his barony with an iron hand may be overdrawn. He was in reality a hardworking capitalist and entrepreneur in a foreign country whose activities and values reflected the class, national, and ethnic biases of the industrialists of his era. Strictly speaking, Shepherd represented capitalism, not feudalism, in Mexico.

In addition to the Shepherd residence, the Hacienda San Miguel consisted of several buildings and equipment surrounded by a high, stone wall. At the front, next to the "castle," was a dining hall or, more accurately, a refectory. Evidently the workers' mess hall was segregated by nationality—Americans from Mexicans. There were also dormitories and a swimming tank for employees. Other structures included a general manager's residence, office buildings, a store, two stables for the mules, and the assay office.[15]

Additional buildings housed the mining machinery, much of it transported over the mountains into Batopilas on muleback. Once the ore arrived at the hacienda (also by mule), it was crushed in the stamp mill, went through the amalgamation sheds that involved the use of chloride, sulfate salts, and mercury, and then to the refinery or reducing plant. Eventually leaching replaced the amalgamation process. There was also a cyanide works for recovering gold. A machine shop for cutting and shaping metals and a foundry that could make iron castings rounded out the hacienda works.[16]

The corrals within the hacienda were spacious enough to house over one hundred mules, as well as hay and corn. (The Tarahumaras, who, along with the Yaqui, were an important source of labor for the mines, also grew and supplied the fodder.) A blacksmith's shop and tack rooms were located next to the stables.[17]

The station keeper, also a resident of the hacienda, supervised the entire operation, making certain that the *conducta,* or bullion train, was prepared for the 120-mile trip to Carichí, via layover stations in the Bufa barranca and at Basíhuare. From Carichí, the silver bars would be transported another hundred miles to Chihuahua City by stagecoach, where, after 1882, the bullion was freighted by railroad to El Paso. Sulfides and silver ore were sent on to Aurora, Illinois, for further smelting. The bullion train tried to average forty miles a day so that the trip to Chihuahua could be accomplished in five days. Tools, supplies, and equipment came back to Batopilas the same way bullion and ore went out.[18]

In the early 1880s, Shepherd obtained permission from the government of Porfirio Díaz to develop all abandoned mines within a sixty-square-mile area of Batopilas. As important, the government allowed him to dam the Batopilas River three miles upstream and construct an aqueduct as well. Water was transported from the dam by way of the aqueduct to the hacienda and the Batopilas mining operations. Underground diversion channels directed the water to Shepherd's residence (which had a bathroom with steam pipes), through the toilets of the dormitories, whence it was expelled back into the river. Water also was channeled to the foundry, amalgamation sheds, stables, and wherever water or power was needed to run the complex.[19]

The aqueduct also brought electricity to Batopilas, the only town in the country outside of Mexico City to have such a luxury. From the aqueduct, water was carried to the Hacienda San Antonio, a reducing plant about half a mile north of the Hacienda San Miguel adjacent to the west bank of the river. Pelton wheels, held up by retaining walls, were rotated by a free jet of water from the aqueduct. The rotors turned six-foot-diameter wheels that produced electricity for the entire complex. The Pelton wheels provided power not only for the mill at San Antonio but also for machinery and air compressors used in drilling. This power also generated lights for the major mine shafts and tunnels. It worked so well that Batopilas had electricity from 1920 to 1940, even though no one in town knew how to attend to the turbines. In 1940, the town was destroyed by a major flood and did not have electricity again until 1989, when once again the original Pelton wheels were put to use.[20]

In 1885, to gain access to the Roncesvalles mine and the workings on the west side of the river, Shepherd started blasting a tunnel from the river to the vein. Later, in lieu of blasting, he used hand drills, which were eventually replaced with power drills when electricity arrived. It was nearly two miles long and wide enough for two narrow-gauge tracks. Being a diplomatic fellow, Shepherd judiciously named it the Porfirio Díaz Tunnel. Excavations in the Díaz

Tunnel continued, connecting old shafts and workings from above so that instead of hoisting ores, they could simply be rolled down to mule cars in the main passageway, from which they went directly to the San Antonio mill at the mouth of the tunnel. The Díaz Tunnel, completed in 1899, was the longest mine shaft in Mexico, reportedly stretching to over seventy miles of underground workings and, by 1902, at the time of Shepherd's death, supplying 96 percent of all ore smelted. It, more than any other Shepherd project, symbolized the "order and progress" of the Díaz era.[21]

But there were costs for political order and economic progress. As Shepherd accumulated capital, he constantly plowed the profits back into the business, making improvements, purchasing equipment, and expanding his operation. The company's dividends were costly, and after 1902 the stockholders received nothing. Shepherd would borrow at high rates of interest to pay off the debts of previous improvements.[22]

Labor was another expense, not only financial but social. Mexican law required that Shepherd maintain a hospital and dispensary for his employees—Americans, Mexicans, and Tarahumaras. Professional doctors and nurses did not come to places like Batopilas cheaply, and the costs of a clinic that dispensed free medical care were very high.[23]

In addition, akin to the situation in other northern Mexican mining districts (such as Cananea and Sonora), employees were comparably well paid. Unskilled labor received 1.25 pesos a day, while ordinary miners received 3 pesos a day. Although the wages paid American workers were undoubtedly higher than those for Mexicans doing similar work, it was not as disproportionate as the biwage system practiced elsewhere. Workers, especially Tarahumaras, did suffer the humiliation of body searches when they left the mines each day, and wages were garnished for credit at the company store. Finally, punishment for stealing or drunkenness was harsh and quick: the local *jefe político* (district chief) incarcerated employees in the company's own jail.[24]

But the greatest social cost may have been the general plight of rural and urban labor as the material benefits of modernization did not filter down to the average peasant or miner. Rural people were often terrorized by priests, *hacendados* (landholders), *jefes políticos,* and Rurales (Díaz police in the countryside) and exploited by foreign entrepreneurs and Mexican loan sharks. Miners and factory workers had no political rights and suffered from poor working conditions and inadequate compensation. Overall, the education, diet, and public health of the lower classes were inadequate. Class conflict and community rebellions could lead to violence against the authorities and eventually government repression. At the height of the Pax Porfiriato, in Tomochi in the northern Sierra Tarahumara, a place the Jesuits knew in the seventeenth century as the "seat of the Devil," the people exploded, a harbinger of the Revolution of 1910.

In December 1891, some of the inhabitants of the mostly mestizo pueblo of Tomochi had a confrontation with the local priest. Some of these people, including their leader, Cruz Chávez, were followers of Santa Teresa—the saint of Cabora (Sonora), a faith healer and mystic. The Teresita cultists soon rebelled against the arbitrary actions of the local *jefe's* nephew and the mayor's threat to subject them to the *leva* (military draft). Weapons were stockpiled. The government, fearing a messianic uprising and learning that some "believers" were ignoring the will of the local *municipio presidente* (municipal president), sent in a security force.[25]

Encounters and skirmishes continued through the end of October 1892. Then some Tomochi mestizos who had been joined by a bandit group, held out in a cave overlooking the town. As the cave dominates the town, it was a strategic area that the Tomochitecos needed to occupy against the army. However, the cave was overrun by federal soldiers on the fourth day of the attack. Although a few *bandidos* escaped, the rest, a dozen or so, were killed. Eventually, the rebellion resulted in the destruction of Tomochi, and the government suffered nearly five hundred casualties.[26]

Between 1892 and 1910, there were thirty-nine uprisings in Chihuahua alone, three in the Tomochi region. On the national scene, the Cananea strike of 1906 pitted Mexican workers against American managers, and between 1907 and 1908, the world marketplace was in crisis. By 1910 the revolution arrived with a fury, especially in northern Mexico. Díaz was forced into exile. The modernization of the Porfiriato was over, at least for Batopilas.

The decline of the Batopilas mines after 1910 was paralleled throughout Mexico. Although demand during the First World War increased prosperity for the copper companies, when combat ceased, mining and its related enterprises decreased production. In 1926, the world market price of silver dropped, and Mexican silver exports collapsed. Lead, zinc, and copper followed in 1929, with output in the mining sector losing half its value between that year and 1932.[27]

However, as early as 1936, the volume of silver exports was once again on the upswing. World War II created the demand the mineral sector needed, as the United States sought to acquire strategic war materials. In 1941, the United States agreed to buy all Mexican production of copper, lead, zinc, graphite, mercury, and cadmium. While wartime demand did not affect Batopilas directly, isolated as it was with only a little over four hundred residents, it did affect the copper works at La Bufa twenty-two miles upstream, a mine that was first claimed by the Batopilas Mining Company in 1893.[28]

In the early 1940s a one-lane road was cut through the mountains and canyons, a distance of sixty-two miles, from Creel to La Bufa. The road, which went through Samachique and Quírare, was completed by 1948. It had been built by mining interests so that heavy trucks could move the copper and iron concentrates to the railhead at Creel. From Creel, the concentrates went to El Paso where the American Smelting and Refining Company would refine it further, capturing some gold and silver in the process. The Bufa Mining Company was in business from 1943 to 1958, and it was this operation that sank the shafts, mined the ore, took the ore to the concentrator, pumped the liquid tailings over the ledge into the canyon below, and sent the concentrates to Creel and El Paso. Devaluation of the peso and pressures from the labor union eventually forced the closing of the mines.[29]

At an elevation of around 3,200 feet, La Bufa is cooler than Batopilas and for that reason had attracted some individuals from "Bato" to live there. In its heyday it probably had a population of 600 to 700, a hotel, a church, a schoolhouse, a jail, and several stores, along with the mining works. By the late 1970s, there were only fifteen families, but the "clean but rustic" hotel, operated then by Señor and Señora Alfonso Dávalos, was still in service. In 1994, the town had been abandoned, and only a few Mexican families shared the area with American expatriates Jeff Chandler (whose residence is the remodeled jailhouse) and my friend and informant, Don Bush. Although the origin of the name "La Bufa" is unclear, it may come from the Italian *buffo,* an opera comic or buffoon who amuses others through tricks and coarse joking.[30]

Construction of a road from La Bufa to Batopilas was begun in 1975 and completed in 1978. It was limited to four-wheel-drive vehicles because of the precipitous switchbacks. Also, it was subject to washouts in summer and rock slides in winter. Once in Batopilas, one still had to hike the three miles to Satevó, or travel by mule or horse to ranchos in the area. In 1990, Peñoles, one of the larger mining companies of Latin America, started explorations in the area and drilled a one-lane road to Satevó. By 1993, the road ran to San Ignacio and from there almost to the state line of Sinaloa. Trucks now go back and forth between Batopilas and San Ignacio every day.

In 1960 Batopilas had 548 residents; by 1989 it had grown to 685 residents. By the 1980s it was considered to be the leading goat producer of the state. Unfortunately, according to national statistics, the municipality of Batopilas has the lowest living standard in the state of Chihuahua. Today, in the 1990s, Batopilas is still a ghost town in the shadows of crumbling mansions and impressive stonework. Yet it is beginning to stir.[31]

The most telling sign of "progress" has been the recent electrification of the town. In January 1989, I was in Batopilas, enjoying the wonderful warm weather of a Bato winter. The town had no electricity, so when moving from house to house at night I had to use a flashlight. Although some families had small generators and butane, most light was by kerosene lamp and cooking was done on wood-burning stoves. Five months later, in June 1989, I returned to find the plaza ablaze with lights. A year later, once again in June, the entire town was receiving electricity derived from a small hydroelectric system that uses the nineteenth-century Pelton wheels of the Batopilas Mining Company. Two years later, in May 1992, I returned to find not only electric lights, refrigerators, and stoves but the curse of television as well. Since then there has been talk of bringing power in from Yoquivo. Thus, in a few years, I have witnessed a change that brought Batopilas out of the mid-nineteenth century to the post-World War II era.[32]

Recently an asphalt plant was opened at Humirá, and government contractors were busy paving the road between Creel and Guachochi. There is some probability that in the future the road from Creel to Sinaloa through Batopilas will be paved. This highway will do to the canyons of the Sierra Tarahumara what the railroad has done to the mountain country. Once again, the pastoral setting and the Tarahumara culture will be the most likely victims of progress.[33]

Another example of recent change came in the mid-1980s. When Batopilas declined as a mining town, it became a tiny commercial hub supplying basic goods and services to the outlying hamlets and ranchos. *Rancheros* would come to town and load up their donkeys and mules with supplies (coffee, flour, tobacco, etc.) before returning to their homesteads. They might also attend to civil or religious duties, or even visit the local clinic. Batopilas was composed of merchants, craftsmen, a padre, some nuns, teachers, municipal authorities, a nurse, and a few guest houses.[34]

Then, after 1984, as a result of drug raids by a combined force of agents of the Drug Enforcement Agency and the Mexican army, marijuana growers retreated from the exposed plains and foothills to the inaccessible mountainous interior of Tarahumara country, especially the region downriver from Batopilas. Opium poppies and marijuana are grown in abundance. One anonymous informant told me that in 1994 the growers were getting four crops of mota a year and could not sell it as fast as they grew it. It is also alleged that practically everyone in Batopilas, from goat farmers to government authorities, is either in the dope business or supplying his or her own needs. The increase in the illegal drug trade is the result of many factors, including the demand market in the United States, but the new road to San Ignacio is certainly one of them. Those trucks that come to and through Batopilas on a daily basis and the several vehicles that are now registered in Batopilas are not transporting only goat skins and mule hides.[35]

Tourism, virtually nonexistent ten years ago, is on the upswing. Part of this is a natural spillover from Party of the Institutionalized Revolution (PRI) tourist promotions in Creel. Batopilas now has motels as well as guest houses. And the granddaddy of them all is the Hotel Riverside (not on the river's side), owned by "Skip" McWilliams of Troy, Michigan (McWilliams also owns the Copper Canyon Lodge, which is located about twelve miles southeast of Creel— not in Copper Canyon). Advertisements for the Hotel Riverside can be found in newspapers and magazines throughout the United States. They describe the hotel as a restored nineteenth-century hacienda "with Gothic arches, shady courtyards and Victorian setting." As of the summer of 1993, it was open and charging US $200 per night, reservations only. In addition, many of the Tarahumaras in the area are furnishing trinkets and crafts for the tourists, who are also provided with tours to the Satevó "cathedral," the hot springs, and the ruins. Such is life in twentieth-century Batopilas.

Yet Batopilas and the Sierra Tarahumara still represent a pastoral West. While the twentieth century is coming to the area in surges, it has not captured the entire country. There are still genuine Indians and real cowboys, even though, as in the United States, some of the Indians are cowboys. Influences from the United States and the Western world keep pushing in on the people of Batopilas, but they have history and tradition on their side. Alexander Shepherd tried to capture them once before, but he was defeated. And the Tarahumara and mestizo cowboy way of doing things still prevails.

Let me give an example by quoting from my field notes.

Batopilas, 25 May 1990

Slaughter at Batopilas

It was early morning in late May in the old silver mining community of Batopilas. The sun struggled to find its way onto the edges of the canyon. The village was still asleep. Only the rooster was crowing; the mule braying; the butcher's dog uttering a yelp. They signaled that it was time—time to slaughter the bovine.

In Tarahumara society animal sacrifice had been practiced since pre-Spanish times. Afterwards the early Spanish miners and Jesuits introduced sheep, goats, and cattle to the Tarahumara, and these were eventually substituted for wild animals. During the curing fiesta, with smoking incense and ritualistic dancing as a backdrop, the Tarahumaras kill a cow, dedicate the blood to the cardinal directions, hang the carcass on a cross on the patio, and cook and eat the remaining meat. Although they are not strict vegetarians, the very act of eating flesh is often ceremonial to the Tarahumaras.[36]

By the nineteenth century bull butchering had become a form of psychological warfare between Mexicans and native Americans. Victor Villaseñor, author of *Rain of Gold,* tells a story about a greedy Mexican miner who owed a steer to the Tarahumaras. He paid his debt to a Tarahumara lad by skinning the steer alive (so as to keep its valuable hide) and then forcing the naked animal to run up the mountain to the Tarahumara's encampment. Seeing an unclad steer struck terror in the hearts of the native family. The mine owner then slit the steer's throat in front of the Tarahumaras, while informing the household that they would no longer be able to use the spring located in the box canyon since it now belonged to him. Today's horror show would not elicit such fears as this was a Batopilas ritual—a ceremony far different from the butchering practices of pre-Columbian Tarahumaras, nineteenth-century miners, or even modern America.

This Batopilas idol was a lean animal, raised in a semiwild state in the deep gorges and narrow plateaus of the barrancas, grazing on the sparse grasses found between the agave, cacti, and wild marijuana. Unlike the cattle found in the feed-lots of Iowa, it had no history of consuming anabolic steroids, corn, and exotic feeds saturated with herbicides and sawdust. It was simply hand-led to the Bato-pilas lamppost to which it was attached the night before, unaware that the halter in this instance would also serve as the hangman's noose. Unlike the industrial North, it was not transported for hours and days along an interstate highway with-out nourishment, water, or rest, only to be deposited in a holding pen outside a Chicago slaughterhouse.

In Batopilas the moment of dying was quick and simple—a blow to the head and a slit throat administered by a skilled butcher-shaman who was aided by a young assistant and four dogs. This Batopilas bovine would not be the victim of mechanized killing; a disassembly line of faceless bloodletters, kill floors, stagnant water, and clanking chains. This sacrificial calf would not be slaughtered by the new high priests of efficiency.

The municipality of Batopilas—a place of part-time prospectors *(gambusi-nos)* with picks and shovels, cowboys and rancheros, gentiles and Christian Tarahumaras, goats and mules, padre and nuns, and petty artisans and butch-ers—was not yet quite ready to join the industrial age, let alone today's world of cybernetics and computers. The people of Bato might yet defeat, once again, those twentieth-century Shepherds with their restored hotels and guided tours. Only time would tell, and time had always been on their side.

CHAPTER FIVE

NEW RAILS TO OLD PLACES

Modernization and Mexicanization

The value of the Chihuahua al Pacífico cannot be accurately known yet. . . . For many, a train ride will be a novelty; for all, this particular one will be unique as it descends from the meseta central, through virgin mountains explored by only a few white men, into the gorge of the Río Septentrión and out onto the cactus-covered Sinaloa foothills, terminating on a great landlocked bay of the Pacific. Its completion commemorates almost exactly four and a half centuries of European occupation and influence.

Florence C. Lister and Robert H. Lister
Chihuahua: Storehouse and Storms

IT WAS 23 NOVEMBER 1910, and a surrealistic event was taking place in Témoris, an ancient religious ground of the Tarahumaras located at the entrance to the Septentrión Canyon. Several wealthy financiers and important politicians had arrived there from Kansas City, Detroit, London, and Mexico City. No less a figure than *el presidente*, Porfirio Díaz himself, was there to dedicate the completion of the transcontinental railroad from Kansas City to the harbor of Topolobampo, Sinaloa's port city on the Pacific.

Díaz had traveled there from Chihuahua City with the guest of honor, Arthur E. Stilwell, in Stilwell's luxurious car No. 100. This classic car brought up the rear of a special train—a 1904 vintage deluxe all-Pullman train with two diners, a bar, and several private rooms that housed everyone from the former governor of Chihuahua and former ambassador to the United States, now Minister of Foreign Affairs Enrique C. Creel and his wife, Angela (daughter of the wealthy Chihuahua patrón don Luis Terrazas), to Lord Monson (representing British investors) and Queen Wilhelmina of the Netherlands.

Following the dedication, a banquet took place on and next to the train. Díaz proposed a toast to Stilwell in which he professed himself much impressed by Stilwell's accomplishments. Stilwell, in his turn, returned the favor by toasting Díaz and pronouncing him "a second Solomon." More toasts, more greetings, more champagne ("J. & F. Martell, or does the señora prefer Marie Brizard?"), dry martinis, tremendous applause, and a menu that included pâté de foie gras *en bellevue*. Finally Stilwell could laugh at the jibes and cruel humor concerning his railroad to nowhere. His English friends could now see that he was no wild dreamer.

Then the dreamer awoke. It was 23 November 1961. And the surreal had become real. It had taken fifty years longer than he had thought. But the dream was now a reality. Still woozy from the lengthy sleep, it appeared that space and time had gone awry. People had always thought he was a romantic visionary. In 1872 he conceived of Topolobampo as a deep harbor port connected to the Atlantic seaboard by way of Austin, Texas. Again, in 1900, when he formed the Kansas City, Mexico, and Orient Railway Company, he dreamed of a trunk line railroad that would go southwest from Kansas City to Sinaloa and the unknown seaport of Topolobampo. And after 1940, when the Mexican government took over the Orient, he was instrumental in making the dream a reality.

The dreamer could now see the events of 23 November unfold. On that day in 1961, President Adolfo López Mateos arrived in Témoris with an official party from Chihuahua. He inaugurated a new route; this was the beginning of a Mexican "northwest passage," a route from Texas to the Pacific Ocean that ran through some of Mexico's wealthiest country.

Was the dreamer Albert Kimsey Owen, or Arthur E. Stilwell, or perhaps Enrique Creel? Maybe the vision belonged to don Juan Trevino, the man appointed by president Lázaro Cárdenas in 1940 to be the general manager of the government-run Orient? In fact, the idea that became reality had been conceived by many dreamers, theorizers, and utopians over a period of one hundred years.

Owen was perhaps the most quixotic of the early visionaries. At midnight in late September 1872, the thirty-two-year-old surveyor and civil engineer looked over the shores of what he would soon call Topolobampo (meaning "Hidden Water" in the native dialect) on the Pacific coast of northern Sinaloa and envisioned a deep-water port that would connect with a railway line that would run from Norfolk, Virginia, through Austin, Texas, to Topolobampo.

Throughout the remainder of the 1870s Owen lobbied and propagandized his idea of a transcontinental railroad that would connect the Atlantic seaboard with Pacific trade centers, through a Mexican port that was shorter by several hundred miles than either San Diego or San Francisco. Mexico, he argued, was a vast region of pastoral, agricultural, and mineral wealth, a land that was destined to become the India of the United States. By 1881 he had incorporated the Texas, Topolobampo, and Pacific Railway and Telegraph Company.[1]

As an adjunct to the railroad project, Owen soon founded a quasi-socialist community on Topolobampo Bay and advertised for colonists. Although at one time the colony attracted several hundred people, it, and the railroad scheme, failed as a result of financial problems, managerial disputes, and a splintering among his followers. Not one mile of track was laid. In 1900 he was forced to transfer his rights to Stilwell, a Kansas City promoter.

In 1900, when Stilwell incorporated the Kansas City, Mexico, and Orient Railway Company, modernization, stimulated by a global industrial revolution, was well on its way in Mexico. To move away from the past, Porfirio Díaz had created the apparatus of a modern state, with its expanded police, administrative, and judicial powers throughout the hamlets and municipalities of Mexico. Commercial agriculture had expanded; mining, such as the Batopilas operation, was increased; and the telephone and the electric tramway had inaugurated major changes in the communications and transportation industries.

Railroad development was spectacular. In 1876, Mexico had 400 miles of track; by 1911, it had over 15,000 miles of track. During the Porfiriato (1876–1911), 80 percent of Mexican railway construction was financed with U.S. capital (most of the rest was British), and Stilwell's operation was no exception. The Mexican Central Railroad, connecting Mexico City to El Paso, was completed in 1884. By 1888, Laredo and Mexico City were linked with an 800-mile line known as the Mexican National Railroad.

More important for Stilwell, Creel's Chihuahua and Pacific Railroad Company joined forces with the Orient, with Creel becoming vice president of the latter. By March of that year, the combined concerns completed a line 140 miles west of Chihuahua at Miñaca (beyond today's La Junta). By 1905, this route extended to Sánchez (7 miles southwest of what became the town of Creel), where, at 8,045 feet, the western descent would begin. Meanwhile Creel had directed the completion of a railway between La Junta and Temósachi, a line that would eventually connect with El Paso through Nuevo Casas Grandes. Additional grading took place east of Chihuahua and northeast of Topolobampo.[2]

Like Owen before him, Stilwell called his road the shortest transcontinental line from any midwestern center and the Pacific, arguing that it was at least four hundred miles shorter out of Kansas City than any other route. Through Topolobampo would enter the exotic goods of the Far East and the South Pacific, to be transported to the industrial centers of the United States. From the industrial east manufactured goods would travel west over his line. Again, like Owen, he and his writers spoke in superlatives about the fertility of the Fuerte Valley (comparing it to the Nile in Egypt) and called the Fuerte River "one vast gold placer mine." They also spoke enthusiastically of the timber resources of Sinaloa and Chihuahua.[3]

The arrival of the railroad in Sánchez and Sisoguichi soon brought many Mexicans and outsiders to Tarahumara country. This resulted in the inevitable conflicts, with many Rarámuri complaining of being dispossessed of their lands. Creel, who at that time was governor of Chihuahua, proposed a "Law for the Betterment and Cultivation" of the Tarahumaras. The point of the law was not to prevent the Mexicanization of lands but to congregate the Indians on communal lands so that they could be educated and "take their first steps on the road to civilization.[4]

One of these first steps was the creation in 1906 of a colony near Sisoguichi to be named Creel, after the governor. The planned settlement of Creel was to consist of 75 percent Tarahumaras and 25 percent Mexicans. A year later, in spite of the original design, over 40 percent of the inhabitants of Creel were Mexicans. Creel was supposed to become an agricultural colony that would bring about rising living standards for the Tarahumaras and, ultimately, cultural assimilation. From this time on, Mexicanization and modernization went hand in hand, as the railroad became the most important symbol of an advancing frontier of settlement and "civilization."[5]

From these beginnings Creel eventually emerged as a railroad hub, the tourist and transportation center of the Sierra, and an important shipping point for minerals and timber. Eventually, as we have seen, from Creel, mule trails, roads, and highways wound through the Sierra Tarahumara, extending the influence of the modern Mexican state and the values of the dominant mestizo culture throughout.

By 1910 many of Stilwell's British backers were becoming concerned over Stilwell's habit of issuing reports instead of dividends. After 1908 the line was in the red, and the Orient was a deficit operation. Capital was running out, and Stilwell had no new sources. The disconnected Mexican segments of the railroad could not cover their operating expenses. By 1909 the Chihuahua and Pacific sold its rights to a British company, the Mexico Northwestern Railroad (which eventually also acquired rights to the line from Temósachi to El Paso). The violence of the 1910–11 Mexican Revolution was the last straw as financial difficulties of the Kansas City, Mexico, and Orient culminated, in 1912, in receivership and the ouster of promoter, visionary, and spiritualist Arthur Stilwell. The dream would have to be realized by someone else at another time.[6]

During the revolutionary era the Orient underwent several receiverships and reconstructions. By 1928 the Santa Fe Railway gained control of the Orient and immediately sold the three Mexican divisions to Benjamin F. Johnston and the United Sugar Company of Los Mochis, Sinaloa. As a consequence of the depression, Johnston, for administrative purposes, combined his operations with those of the Mexico Northwestern Railroad. Because the depression made it difficult to operate at a profitable level, the managers of the Orient soon were looking for a buyer. In 1940 the Mexican government bought up both stock and bonds in the Orient and incorporated the Kansas City, Mexico, and Orient into the National Railways.[7]

In 1942, with the assistance of the United States, a wartime modernization plan was initiated which would develop several new railroads, including the line of the Orient from Sánchez on the continental divide to San Pedro in the west, approximately 155 miles. Under President Manuel Ávila Camacho, surveying and rehabilitation of the mountain section began. Access roads were completed in the area of Témoris, and preliminary grading was started.[8]

In 1954 the private owners of the Mexico Northwestern Railroad sold their interests to the national government. The Mexico Northwestern then became the La Junta-Ciudad Juárez line of the Ferrocarril de Chihuahua al Pacífico, while the old Orient division became the Ojinaga-Topolobampo line. After 1956 construction work intensified. New bridges were built; tunnels were blasted; roads were graded; ties were laid; "elastic" track (involving a continuous weld that provides a safer and quieter ride and is easy to maintain) was laid; and concrete was poured. The mountain section was built mostly with funds that came from the government's Public Works Department (Secretaría de Obras Públicas), with no U.S. monies being directly involved. By November 1961, the line was finished. Owen's dream of a transcontinental line had become a reality. There was now a road that linked Ojinaga on the Río Grande with Topolobampo in Sinaloa, a distance of 583 miles (see map 6).[9]

The completion of the Chihuahua al Pacífico was a modern railroad engineering feat. According to official figures, there are thirty-seven principal bridges on the Ojinaga-Topolobampo line and some smaller viaducts. The longest bridges cross the El Fuerte and Chínipas rivers. Both use steel trusses in the main spans. The El Fuerte bridge is 1,578 feet long and rests on piers that stand 148 feet above the water; the Chínipas bridge is 984 feet long and 295 feet above the river. The construction crew blasted out millions of cubic yards of earth and rock, resulting in eighty-seven tunnels, and, in slide areas, built concrete arches or "false" tunnels. One tunnel runs 4,056 feet under the continental divide; another, El Descanso, 6,035 feet, is the longest in Mexico. At El Lazo, between Creel and La Laja, the railroad forms a complete loop. Construction also included 289 miles of elastic track on concrete or treated timber ties. All in all, the Chihuahua al Pacífico is a railroad buff's delight.[10] This enthusiasm notwithstanding, it is fair and necessary to ask about the effects of the railroad on the society and economy of the Sierra Tarahumara, especially the indigenous population.

In 1940, a majority of the workers recruited for the construction projects were Tarahumaras who had never received a paycheck and were armed only with picks and shovels. By 1961 many of these same individuals were piloting graders and heavy machinery. Before 1961 most tourists, foreign or Mexican, had never laid eyes on a Tarahumara. Since 1961 Tarahumaras have been greeting outsiders with baskets, wooden carvings, and other trinkets.

Map 6. Chihuahua al Pacífico Railroad
Courtesy of Robert H. Schmidt, Jr., International Map Co., El Paso, Texas.

Most important, the railroad, a government project, is one more major instrument of a state policy that calls for the eventual assimilation of the Tarahumara. To quote from the official literature, "the Tarahumara Indians, isolated through the ages by the mountains that until a short time ago, were impenetrable, can become part of the Mexican Nation."[11]

The railroad has also facilitated the Mexicanization of the Sierra Tarahumara. When Creel developed as a railhead in the early part of the twentieth century, roads were constructed which linked Creel to several mining and farming areas. With the roads finished, the first non-Indian settlers moved into the region. Basíhuare, for example, became a mule station that attracted mestizo outsiders who eventually settled there and hired Indians to care for their livestock and cultivate their fields. Mestizos intermarried with Tarahumaras. Eventually the mestizos opened a store, providing the Rarámuri of Basíhuare with easy access to manufactured goods for the first time. When the mines failed, mestizos went into farming and merchandising. Many mestizos became muleteers, thereby linking Batopilas with the outside world. Later in the century muleteers were converted into truckers, as Creel became a railway hub and mule trails became roads and highways.[12] Generally, in the region of the railroad there has been an influx of "white men and women" (non-Indians) who have brought population growth, improved transportation and communication, sawmills, and schools.

Has the coming of the railroad fostered or hurt the cowboy tradition in the Sierra Tarahumara? Obviously, cattle come into Chihuahua City every day headed for the slaughterhouses or for export to the United States through El Paso. Chihuahua, a ranching state that has several hundreds of thousands of Hereford, Angus, and Cebu cattle, ranks first in the production and export of beef. Some come from the stockyards and grasslands that are serviced by the Juárez-La Junta line (this is the gama grass country that once belonged to William Randolph Hearst, Cornelius Vanderbilt, Luis Terrazas, and other members of the prerevolutionary landed elite). Yet most of the animals are raised on the grasslands and plains immediately west of Chihuahua, east and north of the Sierra Tarahumara (e.g., the municipio of Guerrero), the products of large-scale commercial ranching, not small, individual ranchers. The vaquero, or cowboy, has been declining in numbers since 1923 in Mexico and today can be be found only in small numbers in the Sierra.[13]

The Sierra Tarahumara has been and remains outside the major ranching areas of Mexico. Creel is the headquarters of mountain industries, like mining or timbering, not ranching. While the railroad has facilitated ranching in other areas, it has not had a great impact on the industry in the Sierra (other than to inflate the prices of beef). Indirectly, of course, the railroad has brought more Mexicans to the Sierra, some of whom have become rancheros. The mestizo cowboys of the Sierra are ranchers, or more accurately, small rancher-cowboys. These are individuals who own a small amount of land and work a few cattle. Most of the ranching economy is regional, with the hides and beef of cattle being used by the local rancher or his neighbors.

Some Tarahumaras, of course, raise cattle, along with burros, goats, and sheep, and a few of the more acculturated individuals even own and use horses to round up their cattle. Yet these are a minority. While some Indians are cowboys, most rancher-cowboys are Mexicans, and, like the farmers in the region, the mestizos have usurped the best lands for their ranching activities.

If the vaquero is dying out in Mexico and the cowboy is already dead in the United States, he, or at least the rancher-cowboy, remains, albeit in small numbers, in the Sierra Tarahumara. The railroad provides him with supplies and necessities but does not link his modest ranching activity to the larger world. Because he is outside the global economy, he is a part of the pastoral West that still exists in this region of Mexico.[14]

Mention has already been made (see chap. 4) of the mineral traditions of the Sierra. The area has a rich mining history, especially for gold and silver. The twentieth century has seen lead, copper, zinc, and manganese added to the list. Most of the current road building in the Sierra has been an attempt to link the mining fields of La Bufa or Batopilas to the railhead at Creel. The road across the bottom of the Sierra between Batopilas and San Ignacio, built by a mining company, is indirectly the result of the coming of the Chihuahua al Pacífico. If the rail line is the Sierra artery, the old and new roads of the Sierra are its veins.

When the mines fail in the Sierra, as they inevitably do and must, many unemployed miners turn to stock raising and farming. While cotton is one of Chihuahua's leading agricultural products, the state still produces more corn than cotton. Most of the farmers of the Sierra, Tarahumara and non-Indian, are corn farmers. The Mexicans also grow beans, wheat, potatoes, tomatoes, garlic, chile, and sweet potatoes. From the west coast, especially Los Mochis and the Fuerte Valley, come a variety of fruits—cantaloupe, peaches, apricots—and sugarcane. These are transported to and through the Sierra to Chihuahua. In the orchards around Cuiteco and in the highlands in general are apples and apricots; bananas, oranges, and figs are grown in the hot lowlands. So Sierra agriculture, while not as rich and varied as in the Fuerte Valley, does make an important contribution to the state's economy.

Planting ranges from the traditional to the modern in the Sierra. When plowing is required, the Tarahumaras often utilize oxen pulling a wooden plow (both gifts of the Spanish), making holes in the furrow with a digging stick. Many acculturated Tarahumaras and most Mexicans have steel plows. The Mexicans often use horses or mules to pull their plows. One occasionally finds a homestead that has been modernized. Here the farmer employs improved hybrids, fertilizers, and tractors.

The corn farmers of the Sierra, like corn and grain farmers in Mexico generally, are doomed to extinction as long as they seek outside markets for their crops. The rocky, infertile soil and arid climate of the Sierra Tarahumara cannot compete with the relatively flat and well-watered grain country of the United States.[15]

While mining may be the most important economic activity of the Sierra, forestry runs a close second, with Chihuahua being Mexico's leading producer of wood. Main forest products are plywood, cellulose, veneer logs, and railroad ties. The most important wood-producing areas have traditionally been the municipios of Madera, Guachochi, and Guadalupe y Clavo—all in Chihuahua's Sierra Madre.[16]

At the same time that Alexander Shepherd was developing the silver mines of Batopilas, Porfirio Díaz was inviting American capitalists to exploit the pine forests of Chihuahua's Sierra Madre. By 1905, the Río Grande, Sierra Madre y Pacífico (later purchased by the Mexico Northwestern Railroad) had constructed a line from El Paso through Nuevo Casas Grandes to Yepómera (immediately north of Temósachi) to facilitate the removal of lumber and minerals to outside markets.[17]

When Creel became a railhead, the timber industry took on a new life. Later, the completion of the Chihuahua al Pacífico spurred the growth of mill towns throughout the edge of the Sierra. Take, for example, the villages of Celulosa and Anahuac, located about six or seven miles northeast of Cuauhtémoc. Celulosa had been the traditional manufacturing center of cellulose, but its growth was very slow prior to 1961. The village of Anahuac (the Indian name for the valley of Mexico), next door to Celulosa and on the rail line between Chihuahua and Creel, had fewer than 350 inhabitants prior to the completion of the Chihuahua al Pacífico. However, by 1963 it had grown into a community of over 10,000, with a hospital, two public schools, hundreds of residences, and three mills: the Celulosa de Chihuahua, with an annual production in the 1980s of 60,000 metric tons of cellulose; the Plywood Ponderosa de México, the producer of TriPly (a plywood product); and Viscosa de Chihuahua, which, in the 1980s, annually produced over four million kilos of "Texcorta" (an artificial fiber). These factories and others in Chihuahua were part of a larger conglomerate known as Grupo Chihuahua. The basic raw material for these industries was the ponderosa pine that comes from the Chihuahua Sierra.

By July 1991, it was being rumored throughout the Sierra that the chip and cellulose plant at Anahuac was to be closed due to the low price of cellulose and the scarcity of trees, causing the loss of five hundred jobs. At the time it was difficult to know if this was an economic reality or a political ploy by the Mexican government to get backing for a World Bank plan that would finance increased logging of the mesa and canyon country of Chihuahua.[18]

Earlier, during the winter of 1990, word began to leak out that in 1986 Mexico had made application to the World Bank (more correctly, the International Bank for Reconstruction and Development) for financial assistance that would aid the government plan to improve roads and increase logging throughout the Sierra Madre, from the Pima lands in the north to Nayarit in the south, including most of the Sierra Tarahumara. The loan amounted to US$45.5 million. By 1992, $1 million had already been released, and critics of the World Bank loan feared that the rest would soon be freed up. While most of the funds would be used directly in road building and logging, a small amount (3 percent of total funds) was slated for conservation purposes, including environmental impact studies, preservation of endangered species, and development of parks and tourism.[19]

Conservationists immediately began to question both the motives and the purposes of the Mexican government in seeking the World Bank loan. Sierra Club publications questioned the scheme, wondering about the impact of increased timbering on Tarahumara lifestyles and erosion and flooding in the watersheds of the Río Conchos area. They also argued for the creation of a national park in the twenty-three square-mile area of the Barranca del Cobre.[20]

In 1991 symposiums, forums, and public hearings were held on the World Bank proposal, including a January meeting at the University of Arizona and a June gathering at the University of Chihuahua. Native Seed, a nonprofit conservation organization headquartered in Tucson, sought to substitute alternatives to pulping that would develop the Sierra Tarahumara in an ecologically sound way, including ecotourism, the commercial use of nontimber forest resources (acorns, piñon nuts, dried fruits, wild chiles and herbs, etc.), and the development of arts and crafts.[21]

With the approval of the North American Free Trade Agreement in early 1994, it became apparent that the World Bank loan, which was still on hold, was simply the tip of a rather large iceberg. Grupo Chihuahua had managed to receive a $350 million loan from Chase Manhattan, and unsubstantiated rumors were spreading that Italy, Venezuela, Canada, and Brazil were planning to cash in on the free trade treaty by financing additional pulping and logging projects in Durango and Chihuahua. Grupo Chihuahua spent over $500 million replacing its old pulp plant at Anahuac with one of the more modern, computer-driven mills in the world. With an increasing pulping capacity, the new plant would bring further pressure on the Sierra Tarahumara's fragile forests and Rarámuri people.[22] Yet, as of early 1995, the Anahuac facility was temporarily closed, a victim of the global financial market.

Meanwhile the Mexican state has continued its 170-year-long push into the Sierra. In 1825, the government enacted the Law of Colonization to encourage settlement of Mexicans in Tarahumara country and to "instruct and civilize the Indians." The result was the legalization of all titles to lands that had been taken from the Indians and the withdrawal of many Tarahumaras to the interior. Mention has already been made of the 1906 Law for the Betterment and Cultivation of the Tarahumaras and how the community of Creel and the Chihuahua al Pacífico Railroad were used to "civilize" and incorporate the Indians into the national fabric. While the municipio structure has brought state and regional authorities into the Sierra, the recent struggle against narco-traffickers has resulted in the federal army operating throughout Tarahumara country.

The authority of the state can be seen in the person of the municipio police, sector presidents, state government offices, army personnel *(federales)*, and ejido leaders and even in the presence of CONASUPO stores in the countryside. (CONASUPO is a decentralized state agency that buys subsidized crops from the farmers and distributes them at low prices to the rural and urban poor.) While the political authorities may be benign, even at times helpful to the poor, they have seldom preserved and developed the indigenous community.

The most recent threat to the Tarahumaras from the state comes in the guise of the Salinas program to privatize communal or ejido lands. While illegal loggers and narco-traffickers and other "outlaws" have usurped some Tarahumara lands, the state is using the law to privatize lands so that developers can be free to exploit them for private gain.

In October 1991, an "Act of Dislocation" document was delivered by agents of the Ministry of Agrarian Reform to the members of the ejido of San Ignacio de Arareco, near Creel. The intent of the document was to gain control of the land around Lake Arareco for the government and then to promote tourism in the area. The Tarahumaras, who had been disenfranchised in the ejido and were losing their lands, were upset. Over three hundred individuals from San Ignacio marched on the state government offices in Chihuahua City. The state officials, embarrassed publicly by the people of San Ignacio, backed down and eventually revoked the Act of Dislocation. Yet the state is still trying to force the ejido to pave a road to the local airstrip, and San Ignacio's people are currently participating in an "ecotourism" project in which the profits of tourism are supposed to go back to the community. Developing local tourism, while a boon to outsiders and Mexican entrepreneurs, does very little or nothing for the residents of San Ignacio.[23]

But the tourism industry is hitting the Sierra with a vengeance. Again, most of the hotel building has occurred because of the railroad and along the railroad's path. The owners of these hotels are mostly local business people who built hotels after the railroad came. Between Creel and Los Mochis there are several lodges. At the Divisadero is the Hotel Cabañas, built by the railroad in 1974 at a spot that once was a campground on the mule and horse trail from Creel to Chínipas. The hotel is on the edge of the barranca and offers a spectacular view of the Cobre, Tararecua, and Urique canyons. On the Pacific slopes of the Sierra Madre at Bahuichivo there are several hotels, including the Posada Barrancas. At Cerocahui, once the site of Jesuit and Franciscan missions, the Hotel Misión was built in 1976. Continuing twelve miles out of the Río Cerocahui Canyon, one arrives at the Urique Canyon Cabins, a mountain lodge in the pine forest of the Sierra Madre. Finally, on the way to Los Mochis one can find lodging at hotels in El Fuerte.

Creel, of course, is the tourist center of the Sierra Tarahumara. It is also the jumping-off place to La Bufa and Batopilas. In 1962, one year after the transcontinental railroad was completed, the Hotel Nuevo was built by a Spanish teacher. Another landmark, the Hotel Parador de la Montaña, was opened in 1973. As indicated previously, the owners of the Copper Canyon Lodge (a few miles outside of Creel) have recently opened a sister hotel in Batopilas, known as La Hacienda Batopilas Hotel or Hotel Riverside.

The early 1990s have witnessed a variety of changes in and about Creel. The state government has targeted Creel as an area in which tourism is to be promoted. The plaza has been upgraded, concrete has been poured for the sidewalks, stores have built new facades, and street lighting has been improved. Recently a Texan built a 120-seat, American-style restaurant and lounge. The same person also bought the old ejido-owned Hotel Chávez and converted it into a bed-and-breakfast. Other pensions have opened, and the traditional Casa de Huespedes (guest house) has been greatly expanded. In addition, a sixty-room motel has been constructed with an indoor *palapa* (cabaña) and Olympic-sized pool. And, of course, Creel's citizens can now brag that its main street has both a pizza joint and a hamburger hangout. All of this in a place where, until a few years ago, it was difficult for a tourist to find even a cold beer. Creel means Jesuits; it means the Tarahumara clinic; it means a railroad center; and it means tourists and tourism![24]

When tourists get off the train in Creel, they expect to find Tarahumaras. While looking for Tarahumaras or hiring a guide for rubbernecking, there is always shopping. The mestizo merchants of Creel have opened dozens of curio shops. Some of the products of these shops come from Tarahumaras who make exchanges with the shop owners. However, in some instances, the mestizo merchants have found it more profitable to make their own "indigenous" goods, from violins to wooden *bolas* (balls). Of course, the tourist trade spills over the international border: many American merchants, armed with four-wheelers and a degree in archaeology, comb the hills of the Sierra Tarahumara, hoping to buy artisan goods directly from the natives that will reap large profits in Tucson, El Paso, and elsewhere.

At the mission store at the Creel plaza, tourists can arm themselves with Sierra literature and native wares. Here the tourist can purchase one of several self-published books written and illustrated by Richard Fisher. With Fisher as personal mentor and adviser, one can explore the wonderful scenery of the Sierra through the magic of color photography. Travelers may even choose to participate in Fisher's sport of canyoneering (even if the reader's credulity is tested by the author's claim that his accomplishments are equal to those of Carl Lumholtz). The mission store also has Tarahumara language books, histories, guidebooks, and religious literature. Tarahumara crafts, including Indian dolls, can also be purchased here.

It was probably inevitable in the era of Salinas-style privatization that the state-owned railroads, the Ferrocarriles Nacionales de México (FNM), which operates the Chihuahua al Pacífico, would seek to privatize some aspects of its rail service (excluding the ownership of locomotives). In early 1994 a group of railroad enthusiasts in Texas got the go-ahead from the Mexican government to run a luxury Orient Express-style service from El Paso and Chihuahua City to Los Mochis. Reservations were to be handled by an American-owned company in the United States.[25]

The South Orient Express, as this new rail company is called, has eight restored cars that have been refurbished with a turn-of-the-century look that includes wood paneling, etched-glass dividers, and brocaded upholstery. FNM locomotives pull the train through its voyage. Tours vary from as short as three days to nine days and range from $995 per person, double occupancy, to $2,299. Of course, if one finds one's purse strings getting tight, there is always the second-class train from Creel to Los Mochis for a few pesos. Así es el progreso en la Sierra Tarahumara.[26]

One kind of progress that has occurred with greater frequency since the mid-1980s has been narco-trafficking in the Sierra, especially in the "Golden Triangle" area in the area of southwestern Chihuahua wedged between Durango and Sinaloa. Here on the edge of the Sinforosa Canyon entire communities (e.g., Coloradas de la Virgen) are controlled by *narcotraficantes*. Some of the Tarahumaras in this area have been dislodged by traffickers who use timber roads to move their goma and mota to Parral and Durango, whence the narcotics travel on the heroin highway to Chicago.[27]

In the Batopilas region some Tarahumaras have complained about having their land seized by narco-traffickers and *pistoleros* (henchmen carrying rifles and pistols). In most cases, it is likely that Tarahumara lands are not being seized (since most dope is grown along arroyos and streams and in canyons that the Tarahumaras do not farm) but that the Indians are being deprived of water sources or prevented from using trails. As with most recent changes in the Sierra, the increase in the drug trade is at least partly related to the transportation revolution that has brought railroads and logging roads to the Sierra Tarahumara; rail cars and trucks can transport goma as easily as goats, mota as easily as corn.[28]

The modernization of transportation facilities and roads has led to other kinds of crime as well. Los Mochis, the end of the Chihuahua al Pacífico route, is near the major cocaine distribution center of Culiacán, Sinaloa, and illegal activity there has spilled over to Los Mochis and the railroad towns. In May 1992, for example, fourteen bandidos held up the Chihuahua al Pacífico passenger train at Santa Niño in the western Sierra. They took all the valuables of the passengers and fled on horseback. In 1993 armed robbers held up the bank in the railway town of San Juanito and escaped on horses. That same year saw highwaymen hold up the CONASUPO truck between La Bufa and Batopilas. Earlier, in the previous year, when two soldiers were killed in Guadalupe y Calvo, the military retaliated by beating and torturing Tarahumara women and children.

When Tarahumaras break Mexican laws they are imprisoned at Guachochi. Sadly, the human rights of Indians in the Guachochi jailhouse are frequently overlooked, as is also the case for many mestizos in the Sierra Tarahumara. While crime is no stranger in the Sierra, the form it has taken lately is reflective of the breakdown of isolation as outsiders and mestizos fight with each other, and with the Tarahumara, over the riches of the Sierra.

The parallels of history are unending. In June 1993, I noticed an article in the Mexico City *News* about the port of Topolobampo. Evidently several American corporations, including Burlington Northern Railways and Mc-

Donald's, have been actively participating in development projects that would link the nations of the Pacific Rim with the eastern United States. The Salinas government was promoting Topolobampo as an alternative to the overcrowded California ports and has been active the last few years in dredging a canal that would allow larger ships access to the port, as well as upgrading lighthouses and signals. Before the year was out, President Salinas de Gortari inaugurated the port. By spring 1994, Topolobampo was being hailed in the United States as a symbol of Mexico's new economic order and the North American Free Trade Agreement.[29]

Train station at dawn, Creel, 1987

Engine 1021, Creel, 1989

Porter Pablo González, Break-time in the dome car,
Chihuahua al Pacífico, 1987

Above: Guarding manna from Fuerte Valley, Ortario Berraza
on train from Los Mochis, 1990

Below: Mealtime on the Chihuahua al Pacífico, 1989

Melons for sale, Creel, 1989

Above: Steward, Chihuahua al Pacífico, 1987

Below: On the road, Chihuahua al Pacífico, 1988

Grazing country, north of La Junta, 1990

Cowhand Jr., Soto family pool hall, Satevó, 1990

Sierra cowboy, La Bufa, 1990

Sierra saddles, 1988

Ranchero Andrés Navarrete on business from Los Mochis to Creel, 1987

The plowman, between Sisoguichi and Bocoyna, 1990

Tractor in the land of mules outside Panalachi, 1990

Logging for the mestizos, between Batopilas and La Bufa, 1990

Arnulfo Soto, bodyguard, Municipio de Bocoyna, 1990

Enrique, presidente municipal seccional, and Gilberto,
agente polícia, Sisoguichi, 1990

Above: CONASUPO, Samachique, 1990

Below: Visión doble (Manuel Limones on right), Batopilas, 1989

169

Creel shopkeeper, 1990

Antonio the olla merchant, Panalachi, 1990

Viejo, Creel, 1988

Oldster, Creel, 1990

Evangelista, Creel, 1989

Antonia, la bonita, Batopilas, 1990

Chica, Samachique, 1990

Fatherless Torres children, between Quírare and La Bufa, 1989

177

The doll, between Quírare and La Bufa, 1989

Above: Dinner in Batopilas, 1992

Below: Hot Dog, Creel railroad station, 1989

Gato of the Sierra, Batopilas, 1990

Perro singular, Creel, 1988

Road on plateau near Quírare, 1992

Mestizo cabin, road to La Bufa, 1990

La Tarahumara de la Sierra, 1992

EPILOGUE

Although almost four centuries of contact among the Indians, Spaniards, and mestizos have brought about changes . . . the basic pattern of settlement, population, and economy [among the Tarahumara] has remained essentially unaltered.

Campbell Pennington,
The Tarahumar of Mexico

THE FIGUEROA FAMILY outside of La Bufa may be typical of today's Tarahumara. This is a ranchería household that consists of a husband, his wife, and several daughters and sons. One son has been influenced by tourism. He is extremely handsome, and, like most Mexican youths his age, he hangs around Batopilas attracting women. His behavior, very unlike that of his elders, is very *mexicano*. The Figueroa family has modified its traditional activities to meet the demands of a tourist economy. They still grow corn and raise goats, but the family also produces goods for the market a few miles away in Batopilas. The young daughters create straw baskets. The wife weaves belts. A son-in-law makes Indian drums for the merchants. The father, an artist, sculpts busts to sell to the tourists. The Figueroas are feeling the effects of a money economy, and it is an open question if the integrity of the family will remain intact as a result.

Because outsiders have occupied the most fertile regions, land is limited. Many Tarahumara men, who cannot make a living on their small, barren homesteads, have found it necessary to leave to work in the city. In the process they abandon their womenfolk, who are now forced to do farm work and confront outsiders alone.

In addition, in some tourist centers like the Divisadero, the mestizos are pushing the Tarahumaras out and taking over many of the merchandising roles. Meanwhile the Tarahumara women working at the Divisadero are using the money they earn selling tourist goods to purchase Coca-Cola and other sweet drinks and in the process are developing dental diseases unknown heretofore.

The growing of illegal drugs is also increasing the difficulties of daily life. There have been reports of Tarahumaras losing their lands to goma and mota growers in the Batopilas and Sinforosa Canyon areas. It is rumored that several drug-related deaths have occurred in the Río Chínipas region. At the very least, many Tarahumaras are beginning to accept cash for growing opium and marijuana. From the Rarámuri point of view, they are merely domesticating wildflowers and natural grass, a task not too different from raising corn and squash. But now they are participating in financial exchanges, something their forefathers did not do. Ultimately, this is integrating the Tarahumara into a cash economy and transforming traditional Indian peasants into petty capitalists.

The threats to the traditional Tarahumara culture are many. All of the non-Indians of the Sierra—drug traffickers, churchmen, politicians, loggers, miners, tourists, backpackers, bikers, owners of four-wheelers, soldiers, policemen, railroad workers, rancher-farmers, gringos, Europeans, and Mexicans—are part of the problem. And each of these "outsiders" is capable of introducing new diseases to the Tarahumaras. But these are also the people of the edge, and they cannot be stopped from smoothing out the rough contours of the rims and ledges, as the global economy invades the Sierra Tarahumara.

My own attitudes on the survivability of Tarahumara culture have changed with the times. Initially, in the mid-1980s, I viewed the Tarahumara from afar and considered them to be a kind of pristine people threatened by outside interests. By the early 1990s, I witnessed the electrification of Batopilas, the new road being built from Satevó to Sinaloa, the rapacious behavior of the timber industry, the journalistic hype associated with the drug trade, and the development of the tourist industry. I was certain that these influences would alter Tarahumara society beyond recognition.

Yet by 1995, my views have become less certain. I have come to two conclusions: first, the Tarahumaras of the twentieth century are very different from their seventeenth-century ancestors; second, there is a certain indolence to the people and land of the Sierra Tarahumara. It is not easy to modify the

status quo and bring change to Mexicans who occupy a remote and sometimes hostile land.

To conclude, let me once again quote from my field notes.

La Bufa, 2 January 1995

I have a renewed faith in the fate of the Tarahumara and the "destiny" of the
Sierra Tarahumara. The powers of reconstruction and renewal are as strong as
the forces of destruction. The Sierra has its own inertia and is, in the final analysis, a pastoral, not a hydraulic, West.

For example, roads get started, but just as quickly, because of local politics and
rivalries, they do not get finished. It now appears that the road to San Ignacio from
Satevó will not link up to Sinaloa in the near future. Why? Because políticos and
jefes in Batopilas have nothing to gain by opening up competition with the west
coast. Another example, the timber industry in which global market trends have
recently forced the closing of the Anahuac facility. As for the church, the Jesuits
are all ecumenicals these days and look upon Tarahumara religious practices, not
as evidences of the Devil, but as revelations of a Christian God. This is certainly an
improvement over the eighteenth-century way of doing religious business.

Even the current plight of the Tarahumaras as they face the problems of poor
crops and malnutrition brought on by the recent drought may not be as bad as
advertised. Charitable agencies, the church, and the state are all responding with
relief supplies. While the priests are rightly concerned about a spring famine, the
storehouses in Batopilas are filled with corn. Even though marginal land and limited wildlife resources in the twentieth century make drought a mightier demon
than in past eras, this is not the first time this century that the Tarahumaras have
suffered drought, crop shortages, and malnutrition. As terrible as the infant mortality figures are, especially for individual families, the Tarahumaras are slowly
increasing their population due to medical and health advances.

It should also be noted that the Tarahumara experience has always been one
of change, even before the arrival of the Spaniards, and the contemporary impact
of mestizos on the natives is part of that historical process. Also, modernization is
not only an external force but one in which many Tarahumaras were and are attracted to the opportunities of change. Many Tarahumaras have taken advantage
of development in the region, becoming commercial pilots, drug traffickers, and
even Protestants in the process. Thus the world of the Tarahumaras is being mes-
tizoized, but many of the natives welcome it.

So the Tarahumara record is one of survival. They are not pristine. They have
been affected throughout the centuries. Acculturation yes, but incomplete accul-

turation. Yesterday I met Isidro Figueroa from the Rincón ranchería outside La Bufa. He was wearing on his left wrist a new Timex watch. It was very likely being used for ornamental purposes, even though he swore that he could tell time with it. What greater symbol of technology and scientific management is there than the clock or watch? Yet he will more than likely tire of his new watch and eventually sell it for pesos that will later be exchanged for sugar, salt, and corn—and the corn will be used for the next tesgüinada!

It is to be hoped that Campbell Pennington's observations in the 1960s (which appear in the epigraph to this chapter) still apply today. Will the Tarahumaras be with us four centuries from now? Perhaps, and very likely in modified form, but only if the people of the edge, Indians and non-Indians, talk to their souls and see in their souls a common humanity and purpose.

NOTES

Preface

1. Max Kozloff, "Picturing Mexico in Color," in *México Through Foreign Eyes, 1850–1990,* ed. Carole Naggar and Fred Ritchin (New York and London: W. W. Norton, 1993), 176.

2. Conversation with William Merrill, 16 January 1995.

1. Sierra Tarahumara: Where the Dead Play While the Living Sleep

1. Edward H. Spicer, *Cycles of Conquest* (Tucson: University of Arizona Press, 1962), 29.

2. Geographical information provided by R. H. Schmidt as cited in Richard D. Fisher, *National Parks of Northwest Mexico II* (Tucson: Sunracer Publications, 1988), 30.

3. For nature writing at its best, see Joseph Wood Krutch, *Grand Canyon: Today and All Its Yesterdays* (Tucson: University of Arizona Press, 1958).

4. See Donald Worster, *Under Western Skies: Nature and History in the American West* (New York and Oxford: Oxford University Press, 1992), 19–33.

5. Frederick Schwatka, *In the Land of Cave and Cliff Dwellers* (New York: Cassell, 1893), 274.

6. Grant Shepherd, *The Silver Magnet: Fifty Years in a Mexican Silver Mine* (New York: E. P. Dutton, 1938), 28. In Spanish: *Batopilas: Entraña de Plata* (Ciudad Juárez, Chih.: Impresora Tipográfica, 1966).

7. Schwatka, *In the Land of Cave and Cliff Dwellers,* 217–19.

8. William H. Bergtold, "An Indian of the Sierra Madre," in *Mexican Game Trails: Americans Afield in Old Mexico,* ed. Neil B. Carmony and David E. Brown (Norman and London: University of Oklahoma Press, 1991), 182, 187.

9. Carl Lumholtz, *Unknown Mexico: Explorations in the Sierra Madre and Other Regions,* vol. 1 (New York: Dover, 1987; reprint of 1902 ed.), 212.

10. Schwatka, *In the Land of Cave and Cliff Dwellers,* 236–37; the quote is from Berg-told, "Indian of the Sierra Madre," 187.

11. Bergtold, "Indians of the Sierra Madre," 183.

12. See both Campbell W. Pennington, *The Tarahumar of Mexico: Their Environment and Material Culture* (Salt Lake City: University of Utah Press, 1963), 85–135, and A. Michael Powell, *Trees and Shrubs of Trans-Pecos Texas* (Alpine, Texas: Big Bend Natural History Association, 1988), esp. pp. 37, 48, 50, 59, 71–73, 77, 84–85, 95, 110, 296, 299–300, and 323.

13. Bergtold, "Indian of the Sierra Madre," 192.

14. D. Carleton Gajdusek, "The Sierra Tarahumara," *Geographical Review* 43 (1953): 28.

15. Romayne Wheeler, *Life Through the Eyes of a Tarahumara* (Chihuahua: Editorial Camino, 1993), 31–32.

2. The Rarámuri: Footrunners from the Past

1. An excellent account of the Tarahumara is John G. Kennedy, *Tarahumara of the Sierra Madre: Beer, Ecology, and Social Organization* (Arlington Heights, Ill.: AHM, 1978). For the INI, see 27–28.

2. Campbell W. Pennington, *The Tarahumar of Mexico: Their Environment and Material Culture* (Salt Lake City: University of Utah Press, 1963), 23–24; Kennedy, *Tarahumara of the Sierra Madre,* 26; William L. Merrill, *Rarámuri Souls: Knowledge and Social Process in Northern Mexico* (Washington, D.C.: Smithsonian Institution Press, 1988), 41. Merrill's population figures do not include all Rarámuri, only speakers of the Rarámuri language who are five years of age and older.

3. Kennedy, *Tarahumara of the Sierra Madre,* 96.

4. Compare the somewhat different conclusions of William L. Merrill in *Rarámuri Souls,* p. 31, with John G. Kennedy, *Tarahumara of the Sierra Madre,* p. 12, and Edward H. Spicer, "Northwest Mexico: Introduction," in *Handbook of Middle American Indians: Ethnology,* pt. 2, vol. 1, ed. Evon Z. Vogt (Austin: University of Texas Press, 1969), 777–91.

5. Wendell C. Bennett and Robert M. Zingg, *The Tarahumara: An Indian Tribe of Northern Mexico* (Glorieta, New Mex.: Rio Grande Press, 1976; reprint of 1935 ed.), 356–59; and Merrill, *Rarámuri Souls,* 31.

6. Conversations between the author and Jerome M. Levi, Creel, Chihuahua, 5 June 1989.

7. This listing of aboriginal culture traits that have persisted comes from the discussion in Bennett and Zingg, *The Tarahumara,* 356–68, 384–85.

8. The notion of the ritual four is referred to as the idea of cardinality and is one of four indigenous patterns of life and belief that survived the Spanish conquest iden-

tified by Frances Karttunen in her article "After the Conquest: The Survival of Indigenous Patterns of Life and Belief," *Journal of World History* 3 (Fall 1992): 239–56. The other ideas are duality, reciprocity, and propriety.

9. Thomas E. Sheridan and Thomas H. Naylor, eds., *Rarámuri: A Tarahumara Colonial Chronicle, 1607–1791* (Flagstaff, Ariz.: Northland Press, 1979), 3–4, and Spicer, "Northwest Mexico," 784.

10. Padre Juan Fonte, "Account of Entrada into Tarahumara Country," in Sheridan and Naylor, *Rarámuri,* 9–10.

11. Edward H. Spicer, *Cycles of Conquest* (Tucson: University of Arizona Press, 1962), 28. The other two rebellions occurred much later among the Río Grande Pueblos and the Yaquis.

12. Ibid., 29–33; Sheridan and Naylor, *Rarámuri,* 15–17, 25–30.

13. For an excellent account of the rebellions, especially those of the 1690s, see the description by Padre José Neumann in *Historia de las rebeliones en la Sierra Tarahumara, 1626–1724,* ed. Luis González Rodríguez (Chihuahua: Editorial Camino, 1991).

14. Spicer, *Cycles of Conquest,* 33–37; Sheridan and Naylor, *Rarámuri,* 39–41.

15. Conversations between the author and Jerome M. Levi, Creel, Chihuahua, 5 June 1989.

16. As quoted by William L. Merrill in *Rarámuri Souls,* 49.

17. Merrill, *Rarámuri Souls,* 24.

18. This description is derived from observations made while visiting the Figueroa ranchería near La Bufa, 23 May 1990. Although most Tarahumaras still wear traditional clothing, many women wear cotton skirts sewn from cloth purchased in stores, and manufactured items of apparel, such as jeans and western shirts, are replacing "breeches" and homemade items. Also see Jacob Fried, "The Tarahumara," in *Handbook of Middle American Indians: Ethnology,* Pt. 2, vol. 8, ed. Evon Z. Vogt (Austin: University of Texas Press, 1969), 852–56.

19. Bennett and Zingg, *The Tarahumara,* 371, 386.

20. Monique Cole, "Tarahumara Indians Run Away with the Leadville 100," *Rocky Mountain Sports* (October 1993): 35; Kitty Williams, "Return of the Tarahumara," *Native Peoples* 7 (Spring 1994): 20–27; Carl Lumholtz, *Unknown Mexico,* vol. 1 (New York: Dover, 1987), 282.

21. Kennedy, *Tarahumara of the Sierra Madre,* 54–56.

22. Bennett and Zingg, *The Tarahumara,* 373–75, 386–87.

23. Ibid., 371, 385–86.

24. Bernard L. Fontana (with photographs by John P. Schaefer), *Tarahumara: Where Night Is the Day of the Moon* (Flagstaff, Ariz.: Northland Press, 1979), 111–19.

25. Conversations by the author with Jerome M. Levi, Creel, Chihuahua, 5 June 1989.

26. John G. Kennedy and Raúl A. López, *Semana Santa in the Sierra Tarahumara: A*

Comparative Study in Three Communities (Los Angeles: Occasional Papers of the Museum of Cultural History, UCLA, no. 4, 1981), 54–75.

27. Fontana, *Tarahumara*, 121–52. See also Ginny Guin, "Semana Santa: A Celebration," *Native Peoples* 2 (Summer 1989): 4–10.

28. Merrill, *Rarámuri Souls*, 36–41.

29. Lumholtz, *Unknown Mexico*, 198.

30. Frederick Schwatka, *In the Land of Cave and Cliff Dwellers* (New York: Cassell, 1893), 177.

31. Lumholtz, *Unknown Mexico*, 306.

32. Merrill, *Rarámuri Souls*, 27, 74, 77–79.

3. Cave Dwellers, Padres, and Evangelicals

1. Susan Deeds, "Legacies of Resistance, Adaptation and Tenacity: History of the Native Peoples of Northwest Mexico," mimeographed (forthcoming in the *Cambridge History of Native Peoples of the Americas*), 36. See also the unpublished work by Susan Deeds, "Upheaval and Restructuring: Indigenous Responses to Mission Settlement in Nueva Vizcaya" (forthcoming in *The New Latin American Mission History*, ed. Erick Langer and Robert H. Jackson [Lincoln: University of Nebraska Press]).

2. The best discussion of Tarahumara cosmology is found in William L. Merrill's *Rarámuri Souls: Knowledge and Social Process in Northern Mexico* (Washington, D.C.: Smithsonian Institution Press, 1988), 85–190. "Rarámuri" in this discussion refers to Christianized Tarahumaras. These bautizados, or baptized Tarahumara, distinguish between themselves and the unbaptized ones, or gentiles. The cosmology of the gentiles is even less Christian than that of the bautizados. Merrill's study was based on individuals in the Basíhuare area and may not be representative of the entire Sierra.

3. Ibid., 162–66.

4. Ibid., 172–81.

5. Ibid., 81; Wendell C. Bennett and Robert M. Zingg, *The Tarahumara: An Indian Tribe of Northern Mexico* (Glorieta, New Mex.: Rio Grande Press, 1976), 373.

6. Merrill, *Rarámuri Souls*, 711–76.

7. The cosmopolitanism of the Jesuit order is the subject of Anthony Grafton's article, "The Soul's Entrepreneurs," *New York Review of Books* 41 (3 March 1994): 33–37.

8. In the Opata country of Sonora and northwestern Chihuahua, the Jesuits came into contact with Franciscans whose missionary system spread from Zacatecas in the south to Nuevo México in the north and northeastern New Spain (including central and eastern Nueva Vizcaya, Nuevo León, Nuevo Santander, and Coahuila-Texas). For the political and religious evolution of the northern Mexican frontier, see Peter Gerhard, *The North Frontier of New Spain* (Princeton: Princeton University Press, 1982), esp. map 5b on p. 13 and pp. 19–23 and 167–68. Also see Charles Polzer, *Rules and Precepts*

of the Jesuit Missions of Northwestern New Spain (Tucson: University of Arizona Press, 1976), 24.

9. Campbell W. Pennington, *The Tarahumar of Mexico: Their Environment and Material Culture* (Salt Lake City: University of Utah Press, 1963), 15; William L. Merrill, "Conversion and Colonialism in Northern Mexico: The Tarahumara Response to the Jesuit Mission Program, 1601–1767," in *Conversion to Christianity: Historical and Anthropological Perspectives on a Great Transformation,* ed. Robert W. Hefner (Berkeley, Los Angeles, and Oxford: University of California Press, 1993), 133.

10. The Ortiz Zapata report is reproduced in the Appendix of Peter Masten Dunne, *Early Jesuit Missions in Tarahumara* (Berkeley and Los Angeles: University of California Press, 1948), 235–36. In Spanish: *Las antiguas misiones de la Tarahumara,* trans. Manuel Ocampo (México: Editorial Jus, 1958), 2 pts.

11. Dunne, *Early Jesuit Missions,* 235; Paul M. Roca, *Spanish Jesuit Churches in Mexico's Tarahumara* (Tucson: University of Arizona Press, 1979), 108–9.

12. Merrill, "Conversion in Northern Mexico," 130–33. See also "Cultural Creativity and Raiding Bands in Eighteenth-Century Northern New Spain," in *Violence, Resistance, and Survival in the Americas: Native Americans and the Legacy of Conquest,* ed. William B. Taylor and Franklin Pease G.Y. (Washington, D.C., and London: Smithsonian Institution Press, 1994), 142–43. For the Parral population, see Vincent Mayer, Jr., *The Black on New Spain's Northern Frontier: San José de Parral 1631 to 1641* (Occasional Papers of the Center of Southwest Studies, Fort Lewis College, Durango, Colorado, 1974).

13. Dunne, *Early Jesuit Missions,* 236.

14. Ibid., 235–36; Luis González Rodríguez, *Crónicas de la Sierra Tarahumara* (México: Secretaría de Educación Pública, 1987), 299–300, fn. 16.

15. González Rodríguez, *Crónicas,* 23–41.

16. Merrill, "Conversion and Colonialism in Northern Mexico," 131.

17. González Rodríguez, *Crónicas,* 314–16; Fructuoso Irigoyen Rascón, *Cerocahui: Una comunidad en la Tarahumara* (Chihuahua: Centro Librero la Prensa, 1979), 17–24.

18. Irigoyen Rascón, *Cerocahui,* 22–23.

19. Gerhard, *North Frontier,* 176; Merrill, "Conversion and Colonization in Northern Mexico," 133.

20. González Rodríguez, *Crónicas,* 317–18; Gerard Decorme, S.J., *La obra de los Jesuitas mexicanos durante la época colonial 1572–1767,* vol. 2 (Mexico: Antigua Librería Robredo de José Porrúa e Hijos, 1941), 245. William Merrill reports that the Franciscan missionary Vicente Escalera added to the original structure the bells, various ornaments, finely painted images, and polished statutes, sometime between 1795 and 1802 (Merrill to Raat, Morelia, Michoacán, 24 May 1994).

This church of Santa Angel Custodio de Satevó is not to be confused with the already mentioned San Francisco Xavier de Satevó. The latter is located near the San Pedro River in the Conchos watershed area and was built one hundred years earlier in 1640. The church of San Francisco Xavier de Satevó was still standing in 1969, with two bell towers (one incomplete) and a partially constructed pyramidal top on one of the towers. For the San Pedro Satevó, see Paul Roca, *Spanish Jesuit Churches,* 108–9.

21. Richard D. Fisher, *National Parks of Northwest Mexico II* (Tucson: Sunracer Publications, 1988), 22–28. The same story of the "Lost Cathedral" is found in Fisher, *Mexico's Copper Canyon to the Sea of Cortez* (Tucson: Sunracer Publications, 1989), 32–34.

22. Grant Shepherd, *The Silver Magnet: Fifty Years in a Mexican Silver Mine* (New York: E. P. Dutton, 1938), 50–53. Shepherd reports that one of the bells was cast in Spain before Columbus discovered Española. When I visited the church in 1990 I climbed up to the bell tower and observed three dates—a medium bell on the east side was dated 1720; another medium bell on the south side was dated 1806; and the large bell in the center with the clapper was dated 1801 (cf. my observations with the report in *SMRC-Newsletter* 25:86 [University of Arizona Library, Tucson, March 1991]: 2). Father Luis Verplancken reports that he has witnessed the leftovers from the casting operation that took place on the site (interview of Verplancken by W. Dirk Raat, Creel, 2 June 1992). It is possible that some bells were originally cast in Satevó while others came from outside the region.

23. Gerhard, *North Frontier,* 177.

24. Merrill, "Conversion and Colonialism in Northern Mexico," 138–39.

25. Ibid., 142–48.

26. Ibid., 149–52. For contemporary Sisoguichi, see Jonathon F. Cassel, *Tarahumara Indians* (San Antonio: Naylor, 1969), 43–63. The observation about Judas figures comes from John G. Kennedy and Raúl A. López, *Semana Santa in the Sierra Tarahumara: A Comparative Study in Three Communities* (Los Angeles: Occasional Papers of the Museum of Cultural History, UCLA, no. 4, 1981).

27. Pennington, *Tarahumar,* 16; Gerhard, *North Frontier,* 17, 168; Thomas E. Sheridan and Thomas H. Naylor, eds., *Rarámuri: A Tarahumara Colonial Chronicle, 1607–1791* (Flagstaff, Ariz.: Northland Press, 1979), 102–4.

William Merrill notes that between 1767 and 1830, the Franciscans had more missionaries assigned to the Jesuit mission system than had the earlier Jesuits and during this period invested 75,000 pesos in the construction, repair, and improvement of mission churches. By 1803, they had constructed or remodeled twenty-eight new churches, including Satevó (Merrill to Raat, Morelia, Michoacán, 14 May 1994).

28. The Jesuit rules on native language can be found in Polzer, *Rules and Precepts of the Jesuit Missions,* 17. For the Franciscans in the Conchería, see William B. Griffen, *Indian Assimilation in the Franciscan Area of Nueva Vizcaya* (Tucson: University of Arizona Press, 1979), esp. 51–57.

29. William L. Merrill, "Cultural Creativity and Raiding Bands in Eighteenth-Century Northern New Spain," 133–34.

30. Griffen, *Indian Assimilation,* 99–107. At the same time that some Tarahumara were moving east onto the plains of the Conchería, many of the interior Tarahumaras were retreating from European penetration. By the end of the nineteenth century, the eth-

nic boundaries of the Sierra Tarahumara were withdrawn westward and southward (see map 4).

31. After the Spanish expulsion of 1827 the missionaries in the Sierra Tarahumara were transferred to Alta California, and the twenty Tarahumara missions were placed under the authority of the Franciscan provinces of Zacatecas and Jalisco. Zacatecas took over the northern and eastern missions (Baboroco, Moris, Cajurichi, Guaguachique, Narárachi, Norogachi, Cusárare, Tomochi, Tónachi, and Tutuaca) while Jalisco took over the more western and southwestern missions (Baborigame, Basonopa, Cerocahui, Tubares, Chínipas, Guazapares, Navogame, San Miguel, Santa Ana, and Satevó). Among the new pueblos established by the Franciscans, in addition to Basíhuare, were Munérachi and two visitas of Baborigame—Tierras Coloradas and Guereáchique. See William L. Merrill to W. Dirk Raat, field notes, Morelia, Michoacán, 24 May 1994. See also Irigoyen Rascón, *Cerocahui*, 23–24; interview of Luis Verplancken by W. Dirk Raat, Creel, field notes, 1 June 1990; Merrill, *Rarámuri Souls*, 37.

32. Merrill, *Rarámuri Souls*, 37–38; Carl Lumholtz, *Unknown Mexico*, vol. 1 (New York: Dover, 1987), 202.

33. Gerardo Decorme, *Historia de la Compañia de Jesús: En la República mexicana durante el Siglo XIX*, tomo 2 (Chihuahua: Ediciones Canisio, 1959), 453–60.

34. Manuel Ocampo, *Historia de la misión de la Tarahumara (1900–1965)* (Mexico: Editorial Jus, 1966), 94–95, 177–85.

35. Irigoyen Rascón, *Cerocahui*, 24; Dunne, *Early Jesuit Missions*, 239 n. 3; Decorme, *Historia*, 453.

36. Merrill, *Rarámuri Souls*, 43; Susan Deeds, "Legacies," 38.

37. Interview, Verplancken by Raat, Creel, 30 May 1990 and 1 June 1990.

38. Interview, Verplancken by W. Dirk Raat, Creel, 2 June 1992.

39. Ibid.; see also *Tarahumara: A Cry from the Wilderness* (videotape, Moon Kochis Productions, Farmington Hills, Mich., 1991).

40. Interview, Verplancken by Raat, 2 June 1992.

41. Ibid.

42. F. LaMond Tullis, *Mormons in Mexico: The Dynamics of Faith and Culture* (Logan: Utah State University Press, 1987), xii, 18–19.

43. Ibid., 20–26.

44. Ibid., 26–30, 65–66. For the Mormon prophecy concerning Lamanites and the New Jerusalem, see Bruce R. McConkie, *Mormon Doctrine* (Salt Lake City: Bookcraft, 1966), 32–33, 428–29, 532–33. According to Mormon doctrine, Lamanites are descendants of Laman, a Jewish prophet who came from the Holy Land to the New World. They are of the House of Israel. Today's American Indian is a Lamanite. Their ancestors had forsaken the gospel, and as a result "the Lord God did cause a skin of blackness to come upon them." When the Lamanites receive the gospel and join the community of believers, they will become a "white and delightsome people" who will participate in the building of a New Jerusalem. It is interesting to note that after the 30 September

1978 revelation that gave priesthood to all worthy males regardless of race, wording in the *Book of Mormon* was changed to "pure and delightsome." See Joseph Fielding McConkie and Robert C. Millet, *Doctrinal Commentary on the Book of Mormon*, vol. 1, *First and Second Nephi* (Salt Lake City: Bookcraft, 1987), 355.

45. Tullis, *Mormons in Mexico*, 30, 60–73. For Mormon colonization in Mexico, see also Thomas Cottam Romney, *The Mormon Colonies in Mexico* (Salt Lake City: Deseret, 1938), 49–59, and Florence C. Lister and Robert H. Lister, *Chihuahua: Storehouse of Storms* (Albuquerque: University of New Mexico Press, 1966), 190–99.

46. Romney, *Mormon Colonies*, 178–94, 214–31, 309; Lister and Lister, *Chihuahua*, 220–25.

47. Interview of Dennis James Vanbuskirk by W. Dirk Raat, Creel, 28 May 1990.

48. Dennis J. Bixler-Márquez, "The Migratory Patterns of Two Mennonite Communities in Mexico," *Journal of Borderlands Studies* 3 (Fall 1988): 36–37.

49. For a standard account on colonization, see Harry Leonard Sawatzky, *They Sought a Country: Mennonite Colonization in Mexico* (Berkeley, Los Angeles, and London: University of California Press, 1971).

50. Bixler-Márquez, "Migratory Patterns," 39–43.

51. Interview of Pedro Martin by W. Dirk Raat, Humirá, 2 June 1990.

52. Ibid.

53. Ocampo, *Historia*, 169–76.

54. Interview of Jim Moss by W. Dirk Raat, Creel, 30 May 1990.

55. For an anti-Protestant episode in San Juanito, Oaxaca, see Patrick Oster, *The Mexicans: A Personal Portrait of a People* (New York: William Morrow, 1989), 199–208.

4. The Search for El Dorado

1. Alexander von Humboldt, *Political Essay on the Kingdom of New Spain*, vol. 3 (London, 1811; reprint, New York: AMS Press, 1966), 146; Jack Weatherford, *Indian Givers: How the Indians of the Americas Transformed the World* (New York: Fawcett Columbine, 1988), 14; Carlos Prieto, *Mining in the New World* (New York: McGraw-Hill, 1973), 21–22. For mining in Chihuahua, see Florence C. Lister and Robert H. Lister, *Chihuahua: Storehouse of Storms* (Albuquerque: University of New Mexico Press, 1966), 75–77.

2. Weatherford, *Indian Givers*, 16–17; Prieto, *Mining in the New World*, 24–25; Humboldt, *Political Essay*, 138–39.

3. W. Dirk Raat, *Mexico and the United States: Ambivalent Vistas* (Athens: University of Georgia Press, 1992), 46.

4. Fernand Braudel, *The Perspective of the World*, vol. 3 of *Civilization and Capitalism: 15th-18th Century* (New York: Harper & Row, 1984), 421–22.

5. Peter Gerhard, *The North Frontier of New Spain* (Princeton: Princeton University Press, 1982), 170; Lister and Lister, *Chihuahua*, 75.

Frederick Schwatka, along with a host of recent writers, erroneously reports the date of Batopilas's founding as 1632. It is likely that this date has been confused with the later year, 1732, when Batopilas was upgraded to an *alcaldía mayor*. See Schwatka, *In the Land of Cave and Cliff Dwellers* New York: Cassell, 1893), 319. Cf. Schwatka with Lisa June Hart, "Shepherd's Castle: Documentation of a Gothic Revival House in a Mexican Silver Mining Town" (Master's thesis, University of Texas at Austin, 1988), 13, and Gregg Wilkerson, "Geology of the Batopilas Mining District, Chihuahua, Mexico" (Ph.D. dissertation, University of Texas at El Paso, 1983), 10. Also see Juan Cancelada Velá-quez, *Breve reseña de Batopilas, vida y costumbres de los Tarahumaras* (Mexico: n.p., 1950), 15.

6. For the colonial government of Batopilas, see Gerhard, *North Frontier*, 163, 174–79. Also see Oakah L. Jones, Jr., *Nueva Vizcaya: Heartland of the Spanish Frontier* (Albuquerque: University of New Mexico Press, 1988).

7. Schwatka, *In the Land of Cave and Cliff Dwellers*, 321–22; Hart, "Shepherd's Castle," 14.

8. Hart, "Shepherd's Castle," 15–18.

9. Schwatka, *In the Land of Cave and Cliff Dwellers*, 315–16; Humboldt, *Political Essay*, 123–24, 138–39, 157, 433; David M. Pletcher, *Rails, Mines, and Progress: Seven American Promoters in Mexico, 1867–1911* (Ithaca: Cornell University Press, 1958), 190.

10. For this theme in U.S. history, see Keith L. Bryant, Jr., "Entering the Global Economy," in *The Oxford History of the American West*, ed. Clyde A. Milner II, Carol A. O'Connor, and Martha A. Sandweiss (New York and Oxford: Oxford University Press, 1994), 195–235.

11. Biographical portraits of Shepherd can be found in several places, including Hart, "Shepherd's Castle," 21–27, and Pletcher, *Rails, Mines, and Progress*, 184–218.

12. Hart, "Shepherd's Castle," 28–34.

13. Pletcher, *Rails, Mines, and Progress*, 211–14.

14. The "feudalistic" image is provided by Hart, "Shepherd's Castle," 4–8. For Pletcher's view, see *Rails, Mines, and Progress*, 207–8. Grant Shepherd's book is called *The Silver Magnet: Fifty Years in a Mexican Silver Mine* (New York: E. P. Dutton, 1938). See the photograph of the Hacienda San Miguel between pp. 16 and 17. The Spanish edition of Shepherd's work is entitled *Batopilas: Entraña de plata*, trans. Concepción Montilla de Camú (Mexico: Impresora Tipográfica, 1966).

15. Shepherd, *Silver Magnet*, illus., pp. 16–17.

16. Ibid.

17. Ibid., 61.

18. Ibid., 60–62; Hart, "Shepherd's Castle," 42–44.

19. Hart, "Shepherd's Castle," 34–36.

20. Ibid., 38–40; Pletcher, *Rails, Mines, and Progress*, 198.

21. Shepherd, *Silver Magnet*, 65–66; Pletcher, *Rails, Mines, and Progress*, 197.

22. Pletcher, *Rails, Mines, and Progress*, 211–14.

23. Shepherd, *Silver Magnet*, 66–67.

24. Pletcher, *Rails, Mines, and Progress,* 202–4; Hart, "Shepherd's Castle," 5.

25. The best study on Tomochi to date is Paul Vanderwood's "Using the Present to Study the Past: Religious Movements in Mexico and Uganda a Century Apart," *Mexican Studies* 10 (Winter 1994): 99–134. See also Francisco R. Almada, *La rebelión de Tomochi* (Chihuahua: 1938).

26. Paul Vanderwood (San Diego) to Dirk Raat (Fredonia, N.Y.), 16 July 1989; interview, Paul Vanderwood by Dirk Raat, Vancouver, British Columbia, 3 April 1993.

Vanderwood insists that only a few Tarahumaras were involved in the rebellion, that the rebels included both upper- and lower-class mestizos, and that it is best not to blanket millenarians with labels like "marginal poor" or "Indian."

27. Raat, *Mexico and the United States,* 122–23, 128.

28. Ibid., 128, 152.

29. Interview, Don Bush by Dirk Raat, Creel, 24 May 1990.

30. Ibid. Bush also suggests that the peak overlooking Bufa looks like a "fool's" hat, hence the name La Bufa. This La Bufa is not to be confused with the La Bufa mine in Zacatecas that was discovered in the sixteenth century.

31. Conversations by the author with Jerome M. Levi, Creel, 5 June 1989.

32. In addition to observations recorded in my field notes for the years mentioned, I also received a communication from Don Bush on this topic—Bush (La Bufa) to Raat (Fredonia, N.Y.), 19 June 1993.

33. Bush (La Bufa) to Raat, 19 June 1993.

34. Conversations with Jerome Levi, Creel, 5 June 1989.

35. Much of this information comes from the observations I have made at Batopilas over the years. See also Raat, *Mexico and the United States,* 169.

36. It should be noted that some of the Jesuit padres reported that many Tarahumaras consumed with relish the meat of those domesticated animals that the Europeans introduced to the area. The padre, Peter Masten Dunne, said that the Tarahumaras fled to the hills, "sure of sustenance for a long time to come from the flocks and herds they had driven off the day before." This event occurred in the year 1616. See Dunne, *Early Jesuit Missions in Tarahumara* (Berkeley and Los Angeles: University of California Press, 1948), 74.

5. New Rails to Old Places: Modernization and Mexicanization

1. An excellent short study of Alfred Kimsey Owen is David M. Pletcher's *Rails, Mines, and Progress: Seven American Promoters in Mexico, 1867–1911* (Ithaca: Cornell University Press, 1958), 106–48.

2. A chronology of the history of the Chihuahua al Pacífico can be found in Joseph Wampler's *New Rails to Old Towns* (Berkeley: n.p., 1969), 43–55. The title for this chapter was taken from the title of Wampler's book. See also Wampler's *Mexico's "Grand*

Canyon": The Region and the story of the Tarahamura Indians and the Ferrocarriles Chihuahua of Pacífico (Berkeley: n.p., 1978).

3. See the chapter on Stilwell in Pletcher, *Rails, Mines, and Progress,* esp. 274–76. See also John Leeds Kerr, *Destination Topolobampo* (San Marino, Calif.: Golden West Books, 1968), 37–107.

4. Edward H. Spicer, *Cycles of Conquest* (Tucson: University of Arizona Press, 1962), 40–41.

5. Ibid., 41.

6. Pletcher, *Rails, Mines, and Progress,* 284–95.

7. Wampler, *New Rails to Old Towns,* 50–55.

8. Kerr, *Destination Topolobampo,* 174.

9. The best study of the several concessions and the construction process that make up the history of the Chihuahua and Pacific is Francisco R. Almada, *El Ferrocarril de Chihuahua el Pacífico* (Mexico: n.p., 1971). An official history has been produced by the Ministerio de Comunicaciones y Obras Públicas called *Breve historia del Ferrocarril Chihuahua-Pacífico* (Mexico: Secretaría de Obras Públicas, 1961). A good introduction is the brochure and brief pamphlet prepared by the Chihuahua Pacific Railway Company. It includes maps, statistical data, listings of tunnels and bridges with kilometer postings, and a brief history of the railway. See *Chihuahua Pacific Railway Co., Mexico* (1984).

10. Kerr, *Destination Topolobampo,* 181–92; *Chihuahua Pacific Railway* (brochure and pamphlet).

11. Edwin F. Block, *Railroad Through the Wilderness* (Chihuahua: Chihuahua Pacific Railway, 1963), 9.

12. William L. Merrill, *Rarámuri Souls: Knowledge and Social Process in Northern Mexico* (Washington, D.C.: Smithsonian Institution Press, 1988), 40.

13. See the map on p. 49 of Robert H. Schmidt, Jr., *A Geographical Survey of Chihuahua* (*Southwestern Studies* monograph 37, El Paso, Texas, 1973).

14. Richard W. Slatta, *Cowboys of the Americas* (New Haven and London: Yale University Press, 1990), 177–78. Slatta notes that Chihuahua had 396,000 cattle in 1902. These were reduced about 75 percent by 1923 due to the destruction wrought by the revolution.

15. Robert Collier, "Future Looks Grim for Mexican Corn Farmers," *San Francisco Chronicle* (28 June 1994), reproduced in *Mexico NewsPak* 2 (4–17 July 1994): 3.

16. Schmidt, *Geographical Survey,* 50–51.

17. Merrill, *Rarámuri Souls,* 39.

18. Don Bush (La Bufa) to Dirk Raat, 17 July 1991.

19. "Sierra Madre World Bank: 'Development' or 'Logging Project?'" *Seedhead News* 32–33 (Spring-Summer 1991): 1–11.

20. "Banking on Mexico's Forests," *Sierra* 75 (November-December 1990): 98–100.

21. "Treasures of the Sierra Madre: Conference Summary," *Sierra* 75 (November-

December 1990): 4–8; "Sierra Madre Logging Project Update," *Seedhead News* 34 (Fall 1991): 5; telephone conversation between Barnie Burns, vice president of Native Seed, Tucson, and W. Dirk Raat, Fredonia, N.Y., 29 July 1994.

22. *Seedhead News* 34 (Fall 1991): 5.

23. "Sierra Madre Development Update," *Seedhead News* 35 (Winter 1991): 6–7.

24. This account of recent progress in Creel is based on personal observations over the years, as well as information from Don Bush (Bush, La Bufa, to Raat, 6 March 1993).

25. Kevin G. Hall, "Luxury Train Will Soon Travel through Mexico," *Ogden* (Utah) *Standard-Examiner,* 13 February 1994.

26. Information provided by brochure of DRC Rail Tours called "Deluxe South Orient Express to Mexico's Copper Canyon."

27. Alan Weisman, "The Drug Lords vs. the Tarahumaras," *Los Angeles Times Magazine,* 9 January 1994, 10–14, 33–35.

28. Paul Salopek, "Harvest of Violence," *El Paso Times,* 26 February 1989.

29. Tom Buckley, "Sinaloa Port to Play Pivotal Trade Role," *The News* (Mexico City), 14 June 1993; Vincent J. Schodolski and Hugh Dellios, "Dream of Free Trade Loses Luster South of Border as the Hard Facts Sink In," *Buffalo News,* 3 April 1994.

BIBLIOGRAPHICAL ESSAY

This essay deals primarily with books and makes no attempt to be exhaustive. Individuals seeking specific items appearing in periodicals and newspapers should consult the notes.

A word of caution concerning the literature of the Sierra Tarahumara. From the historian's standpoint, the scholarship of the Sierra is still in its infancy. Apart from the Tarahumara, little else has been studied. Archaeology is practically nonexistent. Ethnology and anthropology are better developed. William L. Merrill and John G. Kennedy are doing excellent anthropological work today, akin to the earlier efforts of Wendell C. Bennett and Robert M. Zingg. Robert Schmidt, Jr., is doing for recent Sierra cartography what Cambell W. Pennington did for physical geography a generation ago. Yet, aside from the works of the Jesuit historian Luis González Rodríguez and the state historian Francisco R. Almada, the history of the Sierra Tarahumara remains unwritten. This is especially true for the nineteenth century, an era that is only beginning to emerge in our consciousness as a result of Merrill's recent work in the Franciscan archives in Guadalajara.

Because of the paucity of materials, one should be very careful when approaching popular guidebooks. A good choice is E. M. Hendrick's trail guide, *Caminos Reales in Mexico's Copper Canyon* (Albuquerque: n.p., 1994).

Aids for the study of the Greater Southwest are plentiful. A recent work, edited by Barbara G. Valk, is *Borderline: A Bibliography of the United States-Mexico Borderlands* (Los Angeles: UCLA Latin American Center Publications, 1988). Also see Ellwyn R. Stoddard, Richard L. Nostrand, and Jonathan P. West, *Borderlands Sourcebook: A Guide to the Literature on Northern Mexico and the American Southwest* (Norman: University of Oklahoma Press, 1983). Peter Gerhard's *Guide to the Historical Geography of New Spain* (Cambridge: Cambridge University Press, 1972) is central for the history of colonial Mexico.

For the geography of the Sierra Tarahumara, the best study is Robert H. Schmidt, Jr.'s *A Geographical Survey of Chihuahua* (*Southwestern Studies,* no. 37, University of

Texas at El Paso, 1973). Schmidt has a manuscript in press, *The Sierra Madre Occidental of Mexico*, a study of the physical geography of the Sierra Madre that should be in print by 1995 (Tucson: University of Arizona Press). Schmidt provided the geographical information found in Richard D. Fisher's guide, *National Parks of Northwest Mexico II* (Tucson: Sunracer Publications, 1988), He has also prepared the best maps of the area, *Sierra Tarahumara: Barrancas del Cobre* and *Maps and Guide to the Chihuahua al Pacífico Railroad*. Both are published by International Map Co. of El Paso, Texas.

Many nineteenth-century naturalists and explorers wrote descriptive accounts of the land and the people of the Sierra Tarahumara. Foremost, of course, is Carl Lumholtz, *Unknown Mexico: Explorations in the Sierra Madre and Other Regions*, 2 vols. (New York: Dover, 1902). Frederick Schwatka's *In the Land of Cave and Cliff Dwellers* (New York: Cassell, 1893) is also worth consulting.

Studies of the history and anthropology of the Tarahumara are almost endless. Chapter 1 of Edward H. Spicer's *Cycles of Conquest* (Tucson: University of Arizona Press, 1962) is a brief but authoritative treatment of the Tarahumaras. A good beginning for most readers would be John G. Kennedy, *Tarahumara of the Sierra Madre: Beer, Ecology, and Social Organization* (Arlington Heights, Ill.: AHM, 1978) or Kennedy's *The Tarahumara* (New York: Chelsea House, 1990). Tarahumara material culture is surveyed by Campbell W. Pennington, *The Tarahumar of Mexico: Their Environment and Material Culture* (Salt Lake City: University of Utah Press, 1963). The classic anthropological study remains Wendell C. Bennett and Robert M. Zingg, *The Tarahumara: An Indian Tribe of Northern Mexico* (Glorieta, N.Mex.: Rio Grande Press, 1976).

The best work on Tarahumara religion is William L. Merrill, *Rarámuri Souls: Knowledge and Social Process in Northern Mexico* (Washington, D.C.: Smithsonian Institution Press, 1988). Jerome M. Levi's dissertation was completed too late for this study. It is entitled "Pillars of the Sky: The Genealogy of Ethnic Identity Among the Rarámuri-Simaroni (Tarahumara-Gentiles) of Northwest Mexico" (Harvard University, 1993). A copy can be ordered from University Microfilms in Ann Arbor, Michigan. An excellent Spanish source is Luis González Rodríguez, *Tarahumara: La Sierra y el hombre* (Mexico City: Fondo de Cultura Económica, 1982).

Romayne Wheeler's *Life through the Eyes of a Tarahumara* (Chihuahua: Editorial Camino, 1993) is an attempt to study the Tarahumara using their own words. It is a highly romantic, yet interesting, account of the Rarámuri worldview, religious attitudes, and everyday life. Those interested in Tarahumara herbal medicine should consult *Remedios y practicas curativas en la Sierra Tarahumara*, by Francisco Cardenal F. (Chihuahua: Editorial Camino, 1993). Those Spanish speakers who want to begin learning the Tarahumara language can consult Andrés Lionnet, *Los elementos de la lengua Tarahumara* (Mexico: Universidad Nacional Autónoma de México, 1972), or José A. Llaguno, S.J., *Tarahumar (Adaptación del Método "Assimil")* (Mexico: Obra Nacional de la Buena Prensa, 1984).

A competent work in English on the colonial history of northern Mexico is Peter

202

Gerhard's *The North Frontier of New Spain* (Princeton: Princeton University Press, 1982). Also see Oakah L. Jones, Jr., *Nueva Vizcaya: Heartland of the Spanish Frontier* (Albuquerque: University of New Mexico Press, 1988). The best study of the Indian response to the Jesuits is William L. Merrill, "Conversion and Colonialism in Northern Mexico: The Tarahumara Response to the Jesuit Mission Program, 1601–1767," in *Conversion to Christianity: Historical and Anthropological Perspectives on a Great Transformation,* edited by Robert W. Hefner (Berkeley, Los Angeles, and Oxford: University of California Press, 1993): 130–39.

For church history, see Peter Masten Dunne, *Early Jesuit Missions in Tarahumara* (Berkeley and Los Angeles: University of California Press, 1948). José Neumann's account of the Tarahumara rebellions has been translated from the Latin and edited by Luis González Rodríguez in *Historia de las rebeliones en la Sierra Tarahumara (1626–1724)* (Chihuahua: Editorial Camino, 1991). Another source of primary documents, edited by Thomas E. Sheridan and Thomas H. Naylor, is *Rarámuri: A Tarahumara Colonial Chronicle, 1607–1791* (Flagstaff, Ariz.: Northland Press, 1979). Also see Luis González Rodríguez, *Crónicas de la Sierra Tarahumara* (Mexico: Secretaria de Educación Pública, 1984). Nineteenth-century Jesuit history can be found in Gerardo Decorme, *Historia de la Compañia de Jesús: En la República mexicana durante el Siglo XIX,* tomo 2 (Chihuahua: Ediciones Canisio, 1959). The twentieth century is treated by Manuel Ocampo, *Historia de la misión de la Tarahumara (1900–1965)* (Mexico: Editorial Tus, 1966). For a brief overview of Tarahumara religious history from a Jesuit and liberation point of view, see J. Ricardo Robles, "Los Rarámuri-Pagótuame," in *El Rostro Indio de Dios,* edited by Manuel Marzal (Mexico: Universidad Iberoamericana, 1994), 23–87.

Unfortunately, as noted, the history of the Franciscans in the Sierra Tarahumara has not been written to date. For the Conchería, see William B. Griffen, *Indian Assimilation in the Franciscan Area of Nueva Vizcaya* (Tucson: University of Arizona Press, 1979). Merrill's work on the Franciscans will be published in the future.

While the mining industry in Mexico has been treated by several scholars, a specific history of Batopilas, Urique, Ocampo, and the other mining sites of the Sierra Tarahumara still waits to be done. Florence C. Lister and Robert H. Lister, *Chihuahua: Storehouse of Storms* (Albuquerque: University of New Mexico Press, 1966), do cover Chihuahua mining in general.

Alexander Shepherd's son, Grant, wrote about his father's operation in Batopilas. The English version is called *The Silver Magnet: Fifty Years in a Mexican Silver Mine* (New York: E. P. Dutton, 1938); the Spanish translation is *Batopilas: Entraña de Plata* (Mexico: Impresora Tipográfica, 1966). Chapter 6 of David M. Pletcher, *Rails, Mines, and Progress: Seven American Promoters in Mexico, 1867–1911* (Ithaca: Cornell University Press, 1958), is a biography of Alexander Shepherd. An interesting account of Shepherd's money raising techniques and promotional activity can be found in Katherine S. Howe's article, "The Batopilas Flask: A Nineteenth-Century Tale of Money, Mines, and Silver Manufacture," *Winterthur Portfolio* 23 (1988): 63–77. Also see Lisa June Hart, "Shepherd's Castle: Documentation of a Gothic Revival House in a Mexican Silver Mining Town" (Master's thesis, University of Texas at Austin, 1988).

Photographs and news clippings of Alexander Shepherd's Batopilas operation can be found at the Historical Society of Washington, D.C. The manuscript collection at the Library of Congress also has a file, including diaries, on the Shepherd family. Other photographs can be found in the Special Collection of the General Library at the University of New Mexico in Albuquerque.

For railroad history, a good chronology is Joseph Wampler's *New Rails to Old Towns* (Berkeley: n.p., 1969). John Leeds Kerr's book *Destination Topolobampo* (San Marino, Calif.: Golden West Books, 1968) is a complete, if uncritical, history of the Chihuahua al Pacífico. Chapters 4 and 8 of Pletcher's *Rails, Mines, and Progress* are excellent short studies of railroad promoters Alfred Kimsey Owen and Arthur E. Stilwell, respectively. The best work remains Francisco R. Almada, *El Ferrocarril de Chihuahua al Pacífico* (Mexico: n.p., 1971).

For color photography of the Tarahumara, see Bernard L. Fontana, with photographs by John P. Schaefer, *Tarahumara: Where Night is the Day of the Moon* (Flagstaff, Ariz.: Northland Press, 1981). An excellent collection of photographs of Mexico generally is *México Through Foreign Eyes, 1850–1990* (New York and London: W. W. Norton, 1993), edited by Carole Naggar and Fred Ritchin. This latter work contains Carl Lumholtz's 1892 photographs of Tarahumaras and Huicholes. Video copies of film taken by Robert Zingg from his fieldwork in the Sierra Tarahumara in 1935 are available in the Human Studies Film Archives of the Smithsonian Institution in Washington, D.C.

INDEX